Do it  The Lazy Way

 W9-AJU-412

alpha books

LAZY TIPS FOR BUSY PEOPLE

- Use flash cards to learn vocabulary. Be sure to include the noun's gender and plural form on one side. If you are a visual learner, color code your cards with pink for feminine, white for neuter, and blue for masculine. It'll help things stick!

- Note that all nouns in German are capitalized. Always. What could be lazier than recognizing a noun in German? Just look for the capitalized words, and you've found them.

- Like those long German words? German compound nouns are super lazy: they are just individual nouns stuck together. You'll see them everywhere once you start looking. The gender of the last word determines the gender of the new compound.

- Don't know what something is called in German? When in doubt, call it das Dingsbum. You'll get bonus points for your arcane vocabulary, and nobody will be the wiser!

- Look into the history of the English language to see similarities to German. We've lost many over time, but we still have remnants in familiar Shakespearean language: Hath and hat really sound alike, don't they? That's because they're related.

- Don't let those few new letters in German confuse you.

    Never think ß is pronounced like a b because it looks like a beta: it is a double s. An umlaut (those two dots) is really just shorthand for an e following the vowel.

alpha books

*One luxurious
bubble bath*

alpha books

*Access to most comfortable
chair and favorite TV show*

alpha books

*One half-hour massage
(will need to recruit spouse, child, friend)*

alpha books

*Time to recline and listen to a favorite CD
(or at least one song)*

Do it **The Lazy Way**

alpha books

- Make a sign for your front door or office that says *Wir sprechen Deutsch* or *Willkommen*, and see who stops by. You might be surprised.

- We all fumble through life, and some days are harder than others. Traveling can intensify the clumsiness in anyone. Just say "Hoppla," the German equivalent of "Oops," and any passerby will just think you are a German klutz!

- You can save a lot of words by putting as much meaning as possible into your intonation. Like the English words "yes" and "but," the German *ja* and *aber* have a wide range of meanings, allowing one to be facetious, snide, ironic, silly, or serious, depending on the tone. Practice for your best theatrical performance. (And remember to use your eyebrows!)

- Learn how to go undercover in German from a pro: watch a spy movie! Favorites include (from least serious to most serious): *Top Secret*, *Spy Hard*, *Octopussy*, *Shining Through*, *The Spy Who Came In From the Cold*.

- Many tours of castles, cities, or museums are periodically offered in English. Ask when the next tour is available. If you have to wait a bit, enjoy the view or rest your tired feet in a cozy café until it's time to get started.

- Make the countdown to your trip informational and scenic. Buy a calendar featuring your favorite destinations, or load a screensaver of a German map or landmark.

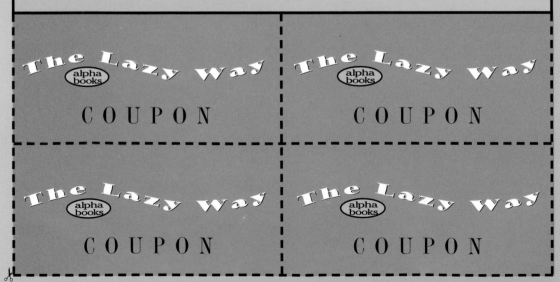

The Lazy Way
alpha books
COUPON

The Lazy Way
alpha books
COUPON

The Lazy Way
alpha books
COUPON

The Lazy Way
alpha books
COUPON

cut

Learn German

The Lazy Way™

Learn German

Amy Katherine Kardel

Macmillan • USA

Macmillan Publishing books may be purchased for business or sales promotional use. For information please write: Special Markets Department, Macmillan Publishing USA, 1633 Broadway, New York, NY 10019.

International Standard Book Number: 0-02-863165-X
Library of Congress Catalog Card Number: 99-61559

02 01 00 99 4 3 2 1

Interpretation of the printing code: the rightmost number of the first series of numbers is the year of the book's printing; the rightmost number of the second series of numbers is the number of the book's printing. For example, a printing code of 99-1 shows that the first printing occurred in 1999.

Printed in the United States of America

Book Design: Madhouse Studios

Page Creation: Heather Pope, Gloria Schurick, John Etchison

You Don't Have to Feel Guilty Anymore!

IT'S O.K. TO DO IT *THE LAZY WAY*!

It seems every time we turn around, we're given more responsibility, more information to absorb, more places we need to go, and more numbers, dates, and names to remember. Both our bodies and our minds are already on overload. And we know what happens next—cleaning the house, balancing the checkbook, and cooking dinner get put off until "tomorrow" and eventually fall by the wayside.

So let's be frank—we're all starting to feel a bit guilty about the dirty laundry, stacks of ATM slips, and Chinese takeout. Just thinking about tackling those terrible tasks makes you exhausted, right? If only there were an easy, effortless way to get this stuff done! (And done right!)

There is—*The Lazy Way*! By providing the pain-free way to do something—including tons of shortcuts and timesaving tips, as well as lists of all the stuff you'll ever need to get it done efficiently—*The Lazy Way* series cuts through all of the time-wasting thought processes and laborious exercises. You'll discover the secrets of those who have figured out *The Lazy Way*. You'll get things done in half the time it takes the average person—and then you will sit back and smugly consider those poor suckers who haven't discovered *The Lazy Way* yet. With *The Lazy Way,* you'll learn how to put in minimal effort and get maximum results so you can devote your attention and energy to the pleasures in life!

THE LAZY WAY PROMISE

Everyone on *The Lazy Way* staff promises that, if you adopt *The Lazy Way* philosophy, you'll never break a sweat, you'll barely lift a finger, you won't put strain on your brain, and you'll have plenty of time to put up your feet. We guarantee you will find that these activities are no longer hardships, since you're doing them *The Lazy Way*. We also firmly support taking breaks and encourage rewarding yourself (we even offer our suggestions in each book!). With *The Lazy Way*, the only thing you'll be overwhelmed by is all of your newfound free time!

THE LAZY WAY SPECIAL FEATURES

Every book in our series features the following sidebars in the margins, all designed to save you time and aggravation down the road.

- **"Quick 'n' Painless"**—shortcuts that get the job done fast.
- **"You'll Thank Yourself Later"**—advice that saves time down the road.
- **"A Complete Waste of Time"**—warnings that spare countless headaches and squandered hours.
- **"If You're So Inclined"**—optional tips for moments of inspired added effort.
- **"The Lazy Way"**—rewards to make the task more pleasurable.

If you've either decided to give up altogether or have taken a strong interest in the subject, you'll find information on hiring outside help with "How to Get Someone Else to Do It" as well as further reading recommendations in "If You Really Want More, Read These." In addition, there's an only-what-you-need-to-know glossary of terms and product names ("If You Don't Know What It Means, Look Here") as well as "It's Time for Your Reward"—fun and relaxing ways to treat yourself for a job well done.

With *The Lazy Way* series, you'll find that getting the job done has never been so painless!

Series Editor
Amy Gordon

Editorial Director
Gary M. Krebs

Director of Creative Services
Michele Laseau

Cover Designer
Michael J. Freeland

Managing Editor
Robert Shuman

Development Editor
Michael Koch

Production Editor
Suzanne Snyder

What's in This Book

DON'T STRUGGLE THROUGH GERMAN, LEARN IT THE LAZY WAY xiv

Sure, there are those children of diplomats who speak all the dialects of Switzerland, Germany and Austria, find the nuances of the German subjunctive quaint and quote Kant in the original, but the rest of us will just have to learn German *The Lazy Way*. With this book you don't have to be an *Übermensch* to understand and speak German. Before you know it, you'll be ready to yodel with joy and ask the natives if it is categorically imperative to like Wagner's music.

Part 1   A Blitz of Basics   1

CHAPTER 1: STRANGER IN A STRANGE LANGUAGE: WHAT YOU SHOULD KNOW BEFORE WE START 3

Look at this chapter as an overview of this strange new tongue you are about to wag, the tools you'll need to tune up your German to high performance standards.

CHAPTER 2: ABCs AND 123s: A GUIDE TO PAINLESS PRONUNCIATION 13

It's kindergarten all over again. (Hey, that's a German word!) But this time it's even easier. This chapter makes pronunciation a breeze with a revolutionary new phonetic system based on common sense and English, the language you already know.

Part 2   When the Going Gets Tough, Get Lazy!   27

CHAPTER 3:   GOING UNDERCOVER: THE ART OF NONVERBAL
COMMUNICATION   29
This is your chance to prove your flexibility, cunning, and human
intuition. By anticipating situations and understanding a few
basics about German culture and customs, you'll be able to do
quite a bit of communicating without words, or at least a minimum of them.

CHAPTER 4:   IF YOU CAN'T JOIN 'EM, BEAT 'EM: CIRCUMVENTING
THE SYSTEM   41
Sometimes it is better to cheat. Or admit you need help. You can
save precious time and money by finding creative work-arounds
to actually having to learn German yourself. This chapter will
show you shortcuts and sneaky tricks that will work in even the
wurst-case scenario.

CHAPTER 5:   SPRACHVERGNÜGEN: HOW TO MAKE IT ALL STICK
51
How do you learn a language? Practice, practice, practice,
right? Well, mostly. But how should you practice? In this chapter
we'll make sure that you have enough ideas about how to have
fun while you are practicing.

Part 3   Sie Sprechen Deutsch?   65

CHAPTER 6:   COGNATES: OLD FRIENDS IN NEW CLOTHES   67
Welcome to the world of cognates, the words that you easily recognize because you already know their English cousins. It's a
small world in many ways. That's why some German sentences
will be obvious to speakers of English. Come and see.

CHAPTER 7: GENDERBENDING THE GERMAN WAY: SEX-CRAZED NOUNS 81

Egaats! There are masculine, feminine and neuter nouns. That is one of the big differences between English and German that causes problems for students of the Teutonic tongue, but I'll show you the easiest ways to deal with this sexy phenomenon and what it means for nouns you'll use.

CHAPTER 8: AN ON-RAMP TO THE ADJECTIVE AUTOBAHN 95

What's a language without descriptive words? Things like the lush, round, curvaceous features of a sweet Bavarian automobile would be indescribable. I'll share the most commonly used adjectives with you and tell you all about declensions. You'll be on the adjective Autobahn in no time!

CHAPTER 9: DO IT IN GERMAN: HAVING YOUR WAY WITH VERBS 109

Don't get tense! We're going to introduce you to the verbs of German gently. We'll start with the most common verbs first, then we'll talk about the differences between the present, past, and future tenses.

CHAPTER 10: WORDWORKS: MAKING SENTENCES 121

Grammar: just the mentioning of the term calls up images of boring seventh-grade English class and diagramming sentences. Forget that. Once you see that grammar is really a coded structure designed to make communication efficient, it will become a favorite tool in your growing "lazy way" war chest.

CHAPTER 11: GUTE MANNIEREN: POISE AND POLITENESS FOR ALL OCCASIONS 133

Granted, Germans have a reputation for being somewhat brusque and barging their way to the front of the line (or European history). But you may be surprised to learn that Germans place a great deal of importance on good manners. You may not be born with continental charm, but once you tackle the three Cs—conversation, customs and correspondence—you'll be the Prost of the party in no time.

CHAPTER 12: DOING DEUTSCHLAND: FROM THE NORTH SEA TO THE BLUE DANUBE 145

Now you're ready to plan your big trip to German-speaking Europe. What will your itinerary include? I'll touch on some of the highlights while showing you some of the key vocabulary and grammar structures you'll need to make your travel communications run as smoothly as a Swiss train schedule.

CHAPTER 13: EXPECT THE WURST: ORDER THE BEST 159

Forget about the nonsense of bad German cuisine. Germany is bursting with regional specialties, and its cuisine has been strongly influenced by Germany's more famous culinary neighbors, France and Italy. Come and see for yourself. I'll tell you the words you'll need to know to find a restaurant in your budget and then order what you like, whether you are a convinced vegetarian or a fan of Hasenpfeffer.

CHAPTER 14: BEYOND BIRKENSTOCKS: SHOPPING AND FASHION 177

German fashions seem a world of extremes—from the clumsiness of sturdy, healthy sandals to the sharp, cold lines of modern designs in black and white. You don't have to be a fashion victim, instead you can express yourself in German—I'll teach you the skills you'll need to confidently shop until you drop.

CHAPTER 15: FROM ALPINE CASTLES TO CHECKPOINT CHARLIE: SIGHTSEEING 193

Whether you want to be an armchair traveler or a frequent flyer mile-earning jet-setter, it's likely that one of the reasons you are interested in learning German is to learn about the sights. And whatever your interests—from medieval torture chambers to bauhaus architecture, from model trains to Alpine lakes—you'll find an interesting way to spend your time while in the German-speaking world.

CHAPTER 16: GUTEN TAG! PLEASANT CONVERSATION 209

Chatting with people in the street or in your train compartment can add a lot of fun to your trip. It can also enrich your relationship with German business partners or extended family. Learn to explore how to use what you already know to get the ball rolling.

CHAPTER 17: THERE ARE NO PROBLEMS, ONLY SOLUTIONS 219

Finding your way out of problems will require you to stretch your language and get creative. When the going gets tough, the tough get going, right? And when things go wrong they generally get tough. I'll show you how to manage everyday problems, real emergencies, and business scenarios.

CHAPTER 18: NOW FOR SOMETHING COMPLETELY DIFFERENT: CELEBRATING IN GERMAN 231

Everyone likes to celebrate, and German-speaking people are world champions at partying, from their famous Oktoberfest to Christmas time celebrations. You will certainly enjoy fun and excitement if you are lucky enough to be present at a German celebration.

MORE LAZY STUFF

A HOW TO GET SOMEONE ELSE TO DO IT 243

You don't have to be a UN delegate to benefit from an interpreter or translator. Learn how to find a qualified language professional to help you cross the language barrier.

B IF YOU REALLY WANT MORE, READ THESE 247

Half the battle is finding the right books, resources and supplies. There are lots of resources for learning more advanced German. Check out this valuable precision German learning equipment if you want more good language information.

C   IF YOU DON'T KNOW WHAT IT MEANS, LOOK HERE 251

Sure, you knew that. *Natürlich!* But here's a quick refresher course in case you don't immediately remember the difference between a direct object and an indirect object, as well as other useful reminders.

D   IT'S TIME FOR YOUR REWARD: ANSWER KEY   255

Here's where you find the answers to the exercises in the book, and to your questions.

WHERE TO FIND WHAT YOU'RE LOOKING FOR   269

Don't Struggle Through German, Learn It *The Lazy Way*

Mark Twain said it would take an educated person thirty years to learn German. Who has decades to dedicate to Deutsch? I can show you how to learn German smarter, faster and easier—in short—how to master it the lazy way! Obviously, Samuel Clemens could have benefited from reading *Learn German The Lazy Way*…

I have heard from many professionals and college students who needed to learn German that their language-learning experience was a struggle. In fact, most people who had German in college remember it as a very daunting experience, full of dry rules and the memorization of useless vocabulary. So who would voluntarily give up their precious free time to submit themselves to this kind of Teutonic torture? Very few people indeed.

That's why I wrote this book. Sure, there are lots of textbooks that promise to teach you German in a few minutes a day, but never before has a book showed you the easiest ways to learn new vocabulary words, shortcuts to help you apply the rules you already know in English and lots of tips and tricks to make your German work for you. By learning German *The Lazy Way*, you'll have more time to enjoy speaking it, plan your trip or just plain get on with your life.

With this book you don't have to be an *Übermensch* to understand and speak German. Before you know it, you'll be ready to yodel with joy and ask the natives if it is categorically imperative to like Wagner's music. The point is that you need to be able to communicate things that interest you and may be important to you personally. If you aren't interested in a particular term or phrase and know you'll never need it, feel free to skip it—your actual progress won't suffer a bit, since it's up to you to decide what will truly be useful for you. And don't worry if there is something that may be important to you personally but isn't covered in this book. I'll also show you ways to learn interesting things that go beyond the scope of this book.

You are the judge of the learning style that best fits you. That's why the very first chapter focuses on assessing your language learning style. Once you've discovered that secret you have won half the battle. The rest of this book is set up to give you the basics you'll need in an easy-to-remember format, including shortcuts, tricks and tips that point out the best and worst ways to spend your time.

My explanations will show you how to learn German smarter, so you can learn it faster and easier. That will leave you more time to philosophize about Kant in quaint cafés, crank off fingertip pull-ups in preparation for your ascent of the Eiger, plan your Alpine driving tour, or just plain relax and watch a rerun of *Hogan's Heroes*.

Dankeschön

The author would like to thank the supportive publishing team at Macmillan, particularly Amy Gordon and Bob Schuman. Special thanks go to Michael Koch for his witty, careful, and timely input as developmental editor. Andree Abecassas proved herself to be an AA agent, and I greatly appreciate her encouragement and support. Thank you as well to Lutz Gollan for his hip German perspective on music and culture. I would also like to express my gratitude to my husband Peter, who helped me make the time to write this book. Finally, I would like to dedicate this book to Andreas Wein and Hilde Häring. They showed remarkable patience while teaching me German as a high school exchange student to Stuttgart. I will always be grateful for their formative efforts.

Part 1

A Blitz of Basics

Are You Too Lazy to Read A Blitz of the Basics?

1 The thought of verb tenses *auf deutsch* make you tense. ☐ yes ☐ no

2 Youareafraidoflonggermansentences. ☐ yes ☐ no

3 You are definitely indefinite about definite and indefinite articles. ☐ yes ☐ no

Stranger in a Strange Language: What You Should Know Before We Start

Look at this chapter as an overview of this strange new tongue you are about to wag. The close, historic relationship between German and English will be revealed at last. You'll come to understand what type of learner you are, how to learn best, and what to learn. You'll also see that there are cases when you can delegate and have someone else do the work for you. Finally, I'll tell you what tools you'll need to tune up your German to high performance standards.

WHAT ARE YOU GETTING YOURSELF INTO?

Today, German is spoken as a first language by almost 100 million people in Germany, Austria, South Tyrol (in Northern

Many of the great works of German literature are available in English translations. You can also find bilingual editions with the German on one page and the translation on the facing page. Although something is inevitably lost in the translation, these books can be a quick way to familiarize yourself with the German poetic mind.

Italy), most of Switzerland, Liechtenstein, most of the French provinces of Alsace and Lorraine, Luxembourg, the Eastern parts of Belgium, and parts of Denmark. German is also likely to be the second language of most Eastern Europeans. These abundant opportunities to speak German make it one of the three most popular foreign languages studied in the United States.

Historically, mathematicians, physicists, and chemists have been required to study German in order to have access to important research in its original language. Musicians and philosophers have long considered knowing German a key part of their curriculum. In today's united "Euroland," there is more reason than ever to acquire the tongue of Europe's economic leader. There is no doubt that the German language will continue to play a key role at the crossroads of an expanding Europe.

ENGLISH AND GERMAN—KISSING COUSINS

The world of languages is divided into families. German and English are both part of the Indo-Germanic family of languages, which means they have common ancestors, such as Great Grandma Sanskrit and Grandpa Greek. German and English are both part of the Germanic branch of the family tree, making them close cousins, relatively speaking.

MASTER IT *THE LAZY WAY*

Over the years, there have been many fads in language learning. It's a bit like the history of dieting—each method touts success with either all eggs, pineapple, or protein, or grammar, conversation, or pattern drills. You don't need to be Dr. Grammatik to know intuitively that a balanced diet of German will serve you best in the long run. Unfortunately, you can neither shed 25 pounds in your sleep nor listen to tapes while you slumber and wake up fluent in German.

A Brief History of the Types of Language Acquisition

The first people to learn German were clergy sent over the Alps to bring Christianity to the heathen Goths around the time of the collapse of the Roman Empire. Even these early travelers were equipped with phrase books of Old High German and Latin. For roughly the next 1,000 years, formal education in foreign languages was grammar based, emphasizing the rules of the language by rote memorization. The practical side of this instruction was considered translation.

As the world got smaller with improved communications technology and transportation, and more and more people needed to communicate in new languages, there was an entrepreneur on the spot to develop a new method of language learning: Maximilian Berlitz. In the late 19th century, he pioneered the *Berlitz Method*, or audio-lingual approach. This meant students would listen to tapes and learn the language without focusing on rules, but rather by listening to "real language." Berlitz was a native German who immigrated to the United States and, in true American Dream style, built a very successful company. He was the first to have only the new

Enjoy a German beer or Swiss chocolate bar and reflect on the great diversity of language on our planet.

The Lazy Way

A COMPLETE WASTE OF TIME

The three worst things you can do when setting your language goals are:

1. To try to do it all at once. Better results come with persistence than with brute force.

2. To set the scope of your learning too broad. Focus on one topic at a time and you'll enjoy yourself more.

3. To forget the reason you're learning German. You'll achieve success faster if you have immediate, tangible rewards.

language spoken in the classroom. It was a radical departure from earlier instruction methods of grammar and translation. In fact, it was much like the way a child learns her first language. Despite its shortcomings, Berlitz's method—and others based upon it—have proven to be extremely popular to this day. Because it takes a great number of hours of exposure to the language to master it, the audio-lingual method certainly isn't the laziest way to learn a language.

Therefore, this book will diverge from the recent trends in language teaching and show you the fastest ways to learn German. By learning and applying a few simple rules, you'll be able to master many situations, rather than memorizing set responses to set situations. I'll even show you how to learn the vocabulary in the Laziest Way possible, in a manner suited to your learning style.

Know Yourself and Your Opponent

Do you really need to learn German? I am not trying to dissuade you from studying German, but in this world where there is so much to know and so little time to learn it all, you need to pick your battles wisely. First of all, there is a big difference between *understanding* German and *learning* German. It is perfectly okay to decide all you need is a passive knowledge of the language so that you can read signs or books in your subject. You might also just want to understand how German works without actually memorizing vocabulary and grammar rules. That's fine, too. There's no call for superhero antics. Your learning experience should meet your needs, not exceed them or miss the mark.

Once you have decided that you need to learn German, the most important questions you should answer honestly are:

- What kind of learner are you?

- What do you want to learn? German for reading? For conversation? How to write a letter to your Oma?

- Why do you want to learn German? For business? For travel? Because it's the only language you don't know?

- How much time a week can you put aside to study?

- Will you have the discipline to work through lessons on your own, or are you better off signing up for a class or making regular appointments with a tutor to keep you on track?

The easiest ways to learn a foreign language are:

- **As a child:** The lack of inhibitions and a biological aptitude that ends after puberty make this the best time to acquire a new tongue.

- **In a foreign country:** Turn your homework into a vacation! If you are willing to immerse yourself in German with almost 24 hours a day of linguistic bombardment, you will learn it the fastest. Look into exchange programs through your school, university, trade organization, or service club. You could also take a course at the Goethe Institut in Germany.

You should remember that there are language professionals who can help you translate a letter or interpret a business presentation. I'll tell you how to find one in Appendix A, "How to Get Someone Else to Do It."

The Lazy Way

- **In an immersion course in this country:** Summer-intensive language programs are available nationally; many colleges and universities offer them. Teens particularly love language immersion summer camps. The most famous is Concordia Language Villages in Minnesota.

- **Among native speakers:** Make friends with, date, or marry a native speaker of German, and insist he or she speak only German with you.

You Don't Need to Learn It All

Part of being efficient in learning German is targeting your vocabulary to your purpose—although in an ideal world you would know more words than you would ever need just to be on the safe side. But that is really the difference between "nice-to-know" and "need-to-know" information. To be efficient, this book will only focus on the "need-to-know" German.

Every learner is going to have different needs. Maybe you are learning German to travel with children. You'll want words such as *der Spielplatz* (playground), *die Windel* (diapers), and *kinderfreundlich* (child-friendly). If you are a wine connoisseur, however, it would make sense to learn words such as *trocken* (dry), *würzig* (aromatic), *Weißwein* (white wine), and *Rotwein* (red wine). Business people will have another list of core vocabulary entirely, including items such as *der Termin* (appointment), *der Bericht* (report), and *der Vertrieb* (sales).

QUICK ● PAINLESS

An old-fashioned pen pal can be a fun way to expand your cultural and linguistic horizons.

Know Yourself—Determining Your Learning Style

What kind of a learner are you? It is important to know your learning style so that you can learn vocabulary and grammar efficiently. Take the following brief quiz and find out the type of learning style that describes you best.

When you need to memorize a phone number, do you:

1. Picture the positions of the buttons on the phone?

2. Write down the number and remember the shapes of the characters?

3. Remember the sounds of the touch tone beeps and dial by tone?

4. Come up with a date in history or a word that matches the number to help you remember it?

5. Memorize the number by the sounds of the words, or do you say it out loud?

6. Not bother to memorize it, knowing it will come to you when you need to dial it again.

You may find that you use more than one of these methods. That's fine; many people have combined learning styles. The three learning styles are as follows:

- **Visual (if you answered yes to 1 or 2):** Visual learners do best by seeing something they need to learn. They will find that using flashcards and writing notes helps them learn efficiently.

QUICK 🔲 *PAINLESS*

Use flash cards to learn vocabulary. Be sure to include the plural form of a noun and its gender on one side. If you are a visual learner, color code your cards with pink for feminine, white for neuter, and blue for masculine. It'll help things stick!

QUICK ◯▢◯ PAINLESS

The more you challenge your memory, the stronger it will become. If learning vocabulary seems impossible at first, remember that it will get more and more painless as you train your mental muscles.

▨ **Audio (if you answered yes to 3 or 5):** Listeners need to say and hear their homework to do their best. They will improve quickly by reading aloud or listening to examples of real language.

▨ **Kinesthetic (if you answered yes to 6):** These are the people who need to do something to learn it. If this is your style, build in activities to your learning routine. For example, if you learn the verb stehen (to stand), stand up. Or learn to count in German while you go up and down stairs.

▨ **Associative (if you answered yes to 4):** This is a contributing method that means you build on what you know. If your style includes a compare-and-contrast strategy, you will benefit from learning grammar rules and how they compare to the language you know—English. You may also find that you will benefit from developing mnemonics or memory aids to help remember words. I'll talk about how the brain uses associations to lock in new information in Chapter 5, "Sprachvergnügen—How to Make It All Stick."

Regardless of the category you find yourself naturally falling into, you can benefit from incorporating the other methods into your routines. The more ways you can reinforce learning, the easier it will be for you to retain and apply your knowledge.

Passive Before Active

It is a given that a passive knowledge of a language (reading and listening) is easier to acquire than an active knowledge (speaking or writing). If you are certain that you need only one kind of knowledge, you can cut corners and hone in on those particular skills. You will find, however, that the skills will complement each other and you will understand each skill more fully if you learn them together. Remember that listening and speaking are natural partners, as are reading and writing. As this chapter ends with a musical interlude, keep in mind how you can combine these skills by reading the lyrics while you listen to your tunes, for example. You'll have them memorized in no time. Just imagine how many style points you'll get when you entertain your party guests with an aria auf deutsch.

GERMAN—IN STEREO!

If you like music, you are in good company with the Germans. Even since before Bach, Beethoven, Mozart, and Handel, the German-speaking world has been a fertile home to musical talent. Whether you prefer your music classical or contemporary, or singers who can rap, waltz, or warble, there is certainly German Musik out there for you. Here's a list of the top of German pop:

Artist	Title
Die fantastischen Vier	*Die da!?!*
Marius Müller Westernhagen	*Freiheit*
Herbert Grönemeyer	*Bleibt alles anders*
Die goldenen Zitronen	*0.30, gleiches Ambiente*
Ideal	*Blaue Augen*

It you are beginning to feel as though learning German is going to be like trying to find your way out of the Black Forest without the aid of breadcrumbs, cheer yourself up by singing along to the video or CD of *The Sound of Music*. (Maybe a talent scout will overhear you and cast you in the sequel.)

The Lazy Way

Artist	Title
Grauzone	*Eisbär*
Kraftwerk	*Das Model*
Die Sterne	*Was hat Dich bloß so ruiniert?*
Peter Maffay	*Und es war Sommer*
Udo Jürgens	*Siebzehn Jahr, blondes Haar*
Fettes Brot	*Jein!*
Helge Schneider	*Katzeklo*
Nena	*Neunundneunzig Luftballons*

Nostalgically inclined listeners might rummage through the racks of their local CD store for those romantic '20s and '30s songs from Marlene Dietrich, Zarah Leander, and the Comedian Harmonists. If you like it folksy, you may want to hunt down those large volumes of traditional German folk music. And, of course, there are Schubert's lieder, Wagner's operas, and Bach's choral music. In short, there is something for everyone's ear. And if you get a tune stuck in your head, you can say "That's a catchy tune" in German: *Das ist ein Ohrwurm!* (Literally, "That is an ear worm!") Visual learners may want to picture a worm crawling out of the ear of a person listening to music.

YOU'LL THANK YOURSELF LATER

While you are working with this book, I urge you to make a list of custom words you think you'll need and to cut those you think you won't need. Go ahead and mark up this book (if it is your copy; librarians don't encourage that sort of personalization).

ABCs and 123s: A Guide to Painless Pronunciation

It's kindergarten all over again. (Hey, that's a German word!) But this time it's even easier. This chapter makes pronunciation a breeze with a revolutionary new phonetic system based on common sense and English, the language you already know. Is it PORSCH or porschE? With these easy rules, you'll fast be able to tackle any soccer player's name or Wagnerian libretto. And while you're learning the first two "Rs," you can cover the third by learning to count. Just so you don't think it's too easy, I'll wrap up by wrapping your tongue around some German tongue twisters.

CONTRARY TO POPULAR OPINION, GERMAN IS NOT A THROAT DISEASE

Well, there is some good news and some not so good news. The good news is that German pronunciation lives up to its

heritage by being logical. There are no silent Es or other tricks to stump you. What you see is what you get. In fact, English speakers will even find that the majority of German vowels and consonants are easy and familiar sounds to the ear.

The bad news is that there are some differences between the pronunciation of German and English vowels and consonants. The differences are really not too bad, however—if you consider that, unlike English, German is very consistent in its pronunciation. And more good news: You don't need to think of German as a throat disease. I'll show you how to tame those guttural fricative consonants of ill repute in this chapter.

VOWELS—SING THEM!

Think of a vowel as a letter you can sing. Technically, a vowel is formed when the air stream flows without impedance through the vocal tract. That means you can hold the *O* in "O Tannenbaum" for two beats. Notice that you can't do that with a consonant—unless you stutter. As a result, vowels are usually the most prominent and central sound of a syllable.

On the next page is a list of the first five vowels in German (which are familiar to us English speakers), plus the three umlauted vowels unique to German.

The Long and Short of It

Each vowel can be pronounced long or short, depending upon its position in a word. The following rules will help you determine the long and the short of it all.

A vowel is long if:

- It is followed by an h (as in *die Bahn*)
- It is followed by an ß (as in *die Straße*)
- It is doubled (as in *das Boot*)
- The letter *i* is followed by an *e* (as in *die Straße*)

A vowel is short if:

- It is followed by doubled consonants (as in *Anna*)
- It is followed by *ck* (as in *der Rucksack*)
- It is followed by *ng* (as in *jung*)
- It is followed by *ss* and *ss* is followed by another vowel (as in *die Messe*)

Having a hard time with umlauts? Try making the sound of a long English vowel (*a*, *o*, or *u*) then rounding your lips slightly as if you're about to whistle. The right sound should come out. When you can do this well, reward yourself by whistling *Edelweiss*.

The Lazy Way

Vowels

Vowel	Short	Long
A	Mann (as in *what*)	Mahn (as in *father*)
E	Bett (as in *ten*)	Beet (as in *may*)
I	in (as in *tin*)	ihn (as in *machine*)
O	hoff (as in *or*)	Hof (as in *go*)
U	muß (as in *pull*)	Mus (as in *cool*)
Ä	Kämme (as in *bet*)	käme (as in *bait*)
Ö	Köln (no English equivalent; almost like *colonel*)	
Ü	München (no English equivalent; almost like *Eew*, in "Eew, yuck!")	

Deutsch, Teutsch! It wasn't until Martin Luther wrote his German translation of the Bible that spelling was somewhat normalized. The word *Deutsch* was originally spelled *Teutsch*. The letters *t* and *d* are not only interchangeable in older German spellings, they often hold the key to their English equivalents. Consider these, for example: *deutsch* (Teutonic), *Tür* (door), and *Ding* (thing).

Diphthongs—The "Twofers"

All the preceding vowels are *monothongs* (Greek for "one sound") and can be made without significant tongue movement during the sound. There are also diphthongs (or "two sounds") that require the tongue to move during articulation. Consider these the buy-one-get-one-free or "twofers" of the German language. While you are holding a vowel sound, you change it into another. Notice this phenomenon when you say "Ouch" in English.

au	Haus (as in *house*)
äu, eu	Häuser, Heu (as in *boy*)
ai, ei	Mai, Fein (as in *fine*)

CONSONANTS—THE PERCUSSION SECTION

Consonants, in contrast to vowels, are formed with some sort of impedance to the air stream. Think of them as the rhythm section of your voice. Each language has a different percussion section and strikes the tongue or vibrates the lips a bit differently. With practice you'll be ready to funk and groove in German in no time.

Say Hi to Old Friends...

These German consonants are very similar to their English cousins: *f*, *h*, *k*, *l*, *m*, *n*, *p*, and *t*. If you listen very closely to German, you will hear a slightly different version of these familiar letters. For our purposes, however, they can be considered the same.

...And Make Some New Friends

There also are some new German consonant sounds to meet. The only two consonants that English speakers will find entirely new are the two sounds represented by *ch*, as in ich or ach. These are the palatal and guttural fricatives that make some ignorant folks think German sounds like a throat disease. It doesn't have to.

The *ch* in ach is pronounced like a continuous *k*, as in the true Scottish pronunciation of *Loch*. It is also very similar to the *ach* sound in the Spanish pronunciation of the Mexican city of *Oxaca*. It is not like an English *ch* or *k*. It should rattle and rasp a bit in the back of your throat but not enough to scare people sitting near you. It occurs after the back vowels of *a, o, u* and the diphthong *au*.

The *ch* in ich is pronounced like a drawn out *h*, as in *humorous*. It should hiss a bit back there in your throat and have a lot of air to it. This sound follows the letters *e, i, ei,* and *ie* (which is pronounced like a long e as in sea).

Another letter in German is just lazy shorthand for a double *s*: *ß* or *Eszett*. It is equivalent to *ss*. Don't let the beta-looking letter fool you; Straße is pronounced like *Strasse*.

Not So Close Consonant Cousins

This last group of German consonants is the group most likely to give English speakers a challenge. Just because they are different, however, doesn't mean they are more difficult. The following straightforward equivalents will get you off on the right foot.

Consonants

Consonants	German Word	Pronunciation
b	Boot, Lob	Like a *p* at the end of a word or syllble; otherwise like its English equivalent.
c	Computer	Like a *k*; seldom used, except in foreign words.
d	Dame, lud	Like a *t* at the end of a word or syllable.
g	Schmetterling	Like a *k* at the end of a word or syllable.
ig	zwanzig	Like the hissing *ich* you learned earlier.
j	ja	As in *yam*.
kn	Knabe	In German the *k* is not silent like in English.
pf, ps	Pforzheim	Both letters are pronounced; no silent p's.
r	Rudolf	Has a bit of a trill in the back of the throat. Call it a "gargle *r*," but don't sound like you are a motorboat. The tongue-rolled *r* is a feature of southern dialects and stage German.
s	So, Stop	Like *z* before and between vowels; like *sh* before p and t. Think *S(ch)tuttgart*.
th	Goethe	In German the *h* is silent.
v	Vater	As in *father*.
w	Wasser	As in *very*.
z	Zoo	As in *bats*.

Stress It!

The one place you do want stress in your life is in your language. *Stress* is the term for emphasis in a word. In German the stress is almost always on the first syllable of a word. There is no rule for foreign words that have been adopted into German. Look them up in a dictionary or ask a native speaker if you aren't sure.

Precision Pronunciation—Brand Names from the Old Country

If you drive a $100,000 car, you should be able to pronounce the name correctly. Otherwise, hand it over! (Just kidding.) Even if you don't own one, boost your consumer confidence by learning to pronounce these brand names correctly. They'll also help you approach the pronunciation of other words you may not know.

Adidas	"AHdeedas"
Audi	"OWdee"
Birkenstock	"BEErkinshtock"
Hugo Boss	"WHOgo Boss"
Porsche	"PORshay"
Mercedes	"MEHRzedays"
BMW	"BAY Emm Vay"
Pelikan	"PELikan"
Pizza Hut	"Pitsah Hoot" (in German: Pizza Hat)
Spaten	"Shpatin"
Volkswagen or VW	"FOLKSVahgin" or "FOW, vay"

Don't let the few new letters in German confuse you.

1. Don't think *ß* is pronounced like a *B* because it looks like a beta. It is a double *s*.

2. Don't ignore the umlauts. Those two dots over vowels can completely change the meaning of some words—for example, *schwul* (homosexual) versus *schwül* (humid).

3. Don't be afraid of consonant clusters; just combine the sounds you know into one bigger sound. German has a lot of examples, particularly in town names like Braunschweig or Pforzheim.

EINS, ZWEI, DREI—WALTZING WITH NUMBERS

Picture yourself in Vienna (or Wien as they say in the city on the Danube, or Donau) at the New Year's Eve ball. You twirl in time to the music and count to yourself: eins, zwei, drei, as you demonstrate your mastery of the waltz to Europe's nobility. Well, it is fun to pretend! But seriously, there are a lot of other times when you will need numbers. Let's dive in.

The Dirty Dozen

With the preceding pronunciation rules, you should be able to pronounce the numbers from one to twelve. The first dozen numbers are the basis for the rest of the German counting system. So, get down and dirty and learn them. You'll get to recycle them later.

0	Null	Nool
1	Eins	Eyns
2	Zwei	Tsvey
3	Drei	Drey
4	Vier	Feer
5	Fünf	Fewnf
6	Sechs	Zeks
7	Sieben	Zebun
8	Acht	Acht
9	Neun	Noyn
10	Zehn	Tsayn

| 11 | Elf | Elv |
| 12 | Zwölf | Tsvölf |

Lucky 13

Starting with the number 13, you'll see a system start to appear. Notice you get to recycle the numbers you've already learned. The digits are in reverse order compared to English. Clearly, the Germans use superior logic in counting. Once you understand the German mathematical mind, the rest is easy. Because Germans are so very logical, they put the smaller number (the one's place) before the larger number (the ten's place), as follows:

13	Dreizehn	Dreytsayn
14	Vierzehn	Feertsayn
15	Fünfzehn	Fewntsayn
16	Sechzehn	Zekstsayn
17	Siebzehn	Zebtsayn
18	Achtzehn	Achttsayn
19	Neunzehn	Noyntsayn

Four and Twenty Black Birds

After the number 20, German mathematical logic continues to apply, but the system changes a bit. Remember that old nursery rhyme about four and twenty black birds baked in a pie? You figured out it was talking about twenty-four, didn't you? Well, Germans use the same system. You just have to recycle the single digits (don't forget to drop the *s* from *eins*) and glue them to the ten base number with the word *und*. After 100, the

QUICK ⬭ PAINLESS

During intense number-based negotiations at a flea market or in a board-room, keep a pen and pad handy to write down figures. It is easy to make mistakes with numbers in a foreign language; with this technique, you can avoid expensive mistakes.

Dot your 1000s and cross your 7s, and you'll avoid confusion. In German notation, one thousand is written 1.000, and one-and-a-half is written 1,5 (and pronounced eins komma fünf). When German speakers write numbers by hand, they cross their sevens, and their ones look a bit like English sevens with a leading upstroke.

und is dropped and numbers are expressed just like they are in English.

20	Zwanzig
21	Einundzwanzig
22	Zweiundzwanzig
23	Dreiundzwanzig

And so on

30	Dreißig
40	Vierzig
50	Fünfzig
60	Sechzig
70	Siebzig
80	Achtzig
90	Neunzig
100	Einhundert
200	Zweihundert

And so on

101	Einhunderteins
102	Einhundertzwei
103	Einhundertdrei

And so on

1,000	Eintausend
2,000	Zweitausend
3,000	Dreitausend

Exercise 1

Write out your own important numbers in German. For example, your telephone number: eins null vier fünf vier sieben zwei.

A friend's telephone number:

_____

Your address:

_____

Your birthdate:

_____

Your high school graduation year:

_____

Practice Makes Perfect

An easy way to practice numbers is to use the German numbers whenever you can. You can talk to yourself, write down phone numbers in German, pick out apples at the grocery store while counting in German, or exercise while counting your reps in German. For an added challenge, try brushing your teeth to a German count. Exercises like these help you internalize the numbers and use them more frequently. And remember: The more you use them, the better you'll be with them! So double up and do two things at once—as long as one of them is in German.

MORE COUNTING ON THE CALENDAR

How many more shopping days until Christmas? Regardless of whether you work in retail, numbers and the calendar will be important when you travel or plan business deals. You'll find the German calendar words

Put on a CD of your favorite German music. Take a bath and count your toes in German.

The Lazy Way

The worst things you can do when scheduling German-style dates are:

1. Forget to put the day in front of the month. (March 4, 1999 is written as 4.3.99.)

2. Not check a calendar for German holidays. There are many more days with no business, banking, or groceries in Europe than there are in the United States.

3. Be late for any appointments. The Germans are unerringly punctual.

very similar to their English equivalents. (And although I haven't yet talked about the gender and nouns, I'll go ahead and introduce you to these nouns. For now, note that the names of months and days are conveniently masculine in German.)

Weekly Grind

Make yourself acquainted with the days of the week:

Montag	Monday
Dienstag	Tuesday
Mittwoch	Wednesday
Donnerstag	Thursday
Freitag	Friday
Samstag	Saturday
Sonntag	Sunday

Calendar Countdown

The months are also very similar in English and German, as follows:

Januar	January
Februar	February
März	March
April	April
Mai	May
Juni	June
Juli	Juli
August	August

September	September
Oktober	October
November	November
Dezember	December

Feiertage—The Calendar's Best Days

The Germans always seem to find an excuse *zu feiern* (to party)—at least that's the impression you get looking at the sheer number of (banking) holidays they have. Here's a list of the most important German holidays:

Feiertage	Holidays
Weihnachten	Christmas
Silvester	New Year's
Ostern	Easter
Oktoberfest	Well, you know this one already

Exercise 2

Fill in the following calendar with the weekdays and holidays for the month of Dezember, 2009.

IF YOU'RE SO INCLINED

Look into the Germanic heroes who gave their names to the days of the week, in both English and German. *Thor* gave us Thursday (*Donnerstag*). *Woden* resulted in the English *Wednesday*. The monkish equivalent Mittwoch (*midweek*), however, was introduced in German as an effort to steer the heathens away from their traditions.

		7	14	21	28
	1	8	15	22	29
	2	9	16	23	30
	3	10	17	24	31
	4	11	18	25	
	5	12	19	26	
	6	13	20	27	

ZUNGENBRECHER—WAG THE MIND WITH TONGUE BUSTERS

Take a crack at the following German tongue twisters.
Don't worry if you can't get them perfectly the first time;
even nimble German tongues have trouble with these.

German Tongue Twister	English Translation
Blaukraut bleibt blaukraut und Brautkleid bleibt Braukleid.	Red cabbage remains red cabbage and bride's dress remains bride's dress.
Ob er über Oberammergau oder aber über Unterammergau kommt, ist ungewiß.	If he comes via Oberammergau or rather via Unterammergau, remains uncertain.
Fischers Fritz fischt frische Fische!	Fisher Fritz fishes fresh fish.
In Ulm und um Ulm und um Ulm herum.	In Ulm and around Ulm and all around Ulm.

If these twisters get your tongue in a knot, remember that Germans have a very tough time with the
English *th* sound. Each language presents its own challenges, and even if your accent isn't perfect, you will still
be understood. Henry Kissinger got a long way with his
heavily accented English; so did Marlene Dietrich. And so
can you, regardless which of these personalities is more
your Doppelgänger.

When the Going Gets Tough, Get Lazy!

Are You Too Lazy to Read When the Going Gets Tough, Get Lazy?

1 Do you think you'd be found out for being a spy before you ever learned the secret handshake? ☐ yes ☐ no

2 Silent treatment? I can handle that assignment. ☐ yes ☐ no

3 Butter on your popcorn? No, that's too much hassle. But I'd like to learn German while I watch a classic film. ☐ yes ☐ no

Going Undercover:
The Art of Nonverbal
Communication

Some of the world's best early silent films came off the lot in Berlin. If Fritz Lang could do it without words, so can you. This is your chance to prove your flexibility, cunning, and human intuition. By anticipating situations and understanding a few basics about German culture and customs, you'll be able to do quite a bit of communicating without words—or, at least, with only a minimum of them.

Body language and dress play a big role in nonverbal communication. Once you figure out how to sneak through without ever opening your mouth, you can complete your disguise as a local. This chapter will give you practical advice on how to "go undercover," negotiate foreign territory, and blend in with the natives. You'll learn tricks they probably taught James Bond in spy school!

Although you can use your index finger to point to your desires, remember not to point at people. It is considered rude.

GETTING WHAT YOU DON'T ASK FOR

There are a lot of situations in which you can successfully manage a task without ever opening your mouth. Think about it: You can easily accomplish simple shopping, restaurant service, or transportation without ever having to talk to anyone. Why? Because you know what you are doing. The same is true for the cool protagonist in a spy movie. What do the two of you have in common? Both of you have a good idea of how to get what you need. You can apply this same system to your traveling language needs by doing a little bit of homework before going to Germany so that you won't have to ask "newbie" questions about the basics, such as transportation, food, and lodging.

General Gestures

Thankfully, body language is relatively similar in German-speaking Europe and the United States. This means that if you don't panic, you'll be able to pantomime quite a few of your needs. This is your chance to be creative; use your imagination to get your point across. These tips will get you thinking about how you can put those hands and head to work while resting your tongue:

Handy Work

Try these handy gestures:

Pointing — Great for indicating items on a menu, choices in a bakery case, or directions to the nearest Biergarten.

Shrugging	The universal response for "I don't know."
Scratching head	Your best impersonation of the thinker.
Tapping head	A gentle tap with the index finger to the temple indicates that not all the cups are in the cupboard.

Heads Up

And remember to put your nodding to work, too:

Nodding	The affirmative response
Shaking	The negative response
Spinning	The universal warning to run for your life

To complete your German gestures training, note that finger counting is different. A thumbs-up indicates one. Then add your index finger for two, your middle finger for three, and so on. You'll look like a native—and get as many of those pastries as you want!

One Word Goes a Long Way

Okay, so you're ready to cheat on your oath of silence. When you do, the one word that may serve you in more instances than any other is *Entschuldigung* (pardon). Use it when you:

- Step on someone's foot
- Want to get around someone on a crowded bus

QUICK ⊂▦⊃ PAINLESS

Don't forget the most important body language of all: the smile. Approach your attempts to communicate with patience and learn to laugh at yourself; you'll be much better received. So put on a happy face!

- Can't hear someone
- Want to get someone's attention

SITUATIONAL SAVVY

Knowing the ropes can make swinging from them a lot easier. If you know what to expect of the situations you will encounter, you can negotiate them without even opening your mouth. Consider this an insider's introduction to the way things work in German-speaking countries, and how to make them work for you.

Trains, Trams, and Automobiles— Transportation Tricks and Tips

Public transportation in Europe is fantastically well designed. Maps and schedules are at every station. This is one time when the Germanic sense of order and punctuality really shines. Reading a train schedule, however, takes an understanding of the system. First, you must find the appropriate map and schedule for your needs. Note that *Abfahrt* means Departures and *Ankunft* means Arrivals. Generally, the posters in train stations are color coded, with departures listed on yellow posters and arrivals on white posters. These posters provide a minute-by-minute and hour-by-hour listing of all trains leaving and arriving at the station and their destinations. They also list the *Gleis* (platform) the trains are using. Larger stations post excerpts of current arrivals on an electronic signboard, which is where you'll see *Verspätungen* (delays) posted. Don't expect many delays, however; trains in German-speaking Europe run like clockwork.

QUICK PAINLESS

Streifenkarten (strip tickets for multiple rides) can save you a bit of money. You just insert the ticket in the validation machine on board the bus or tram and cancel sections of the ticket each time you use it.

Buses, trams, and subways leave from different parts of the main station. Icon signs point the way. Once you find the line you want to take—by referring to a general transportation map—you need to buy a ticket. You can purchase a ticket from an automatic machine in the main areas of stations, or you can buy a ticket on board a bus. The number of zones you travel through determines the ticket price. You can determine the number of zones you need to use by looking at the map.

Now all you need to do is make sure you hop on one going in the right direction. The end destination of a line is clearly displayed on the front. Generally, inside a tram or bus is a map of the route with all the stops listed. On smaller lines, you have to push a button to request the bus to stop for a particular destination. Just watch the signs of the stops and refer to the map, pressing the button for your stop as soon as you leave the previous stop.

If you decide to drive your own car, you'll want to understand some basic traffic rules. And no doubt you'll want to try driving on the Autobahn. (It's true that there is no speed limit on sections of that mother of all freeways!) Ask your local auto club for a brochure on European rules of the road and traffic signs. It'll keep you from scratching your head, missing an off ramp, or getting a parking ticket.

The Best of the Wurst—Being Sausage Savvy

There are some fundamental differences between German and American restaurants. These tips will help you get what you want at a restaurant as easily as possible.

A COMPLETE WASTE OF TIME

The three worst things you can do when driving on the Autobahn are:

1. Pass on the right. The cardinal rule of the road is to pass only on the left.

2. Get in the way of faster cars. It's okay to get in the fast lane to pass, but get back over as soon as you can. Cars may flash their brights at you to move over; they're saying, "Move over, jerk!"

3. Mix it with German beer. Drinking and driving rules are very strict in German-speaking Europe. Don't mix alcohol and the Autobahn.

Naturally, you should pick the right time of day and type of establishment to meet your needs. Note that breakfast in Germany is generally a simple (but hearty) affair of coffee, rolls, and possibly cheese and sausage. You are most likely to find these offered in a *Café* or in a *Bäckerei* (bakery).

Lunch is the main meal of the day and is served in restaurants from noon until about two o'clock. Around four o'clock is time for *Kaffee und Kuchen* (coffee and cake), which are best enjoyed in a *Konditorei* (pastry shop) or a *Café*. Desserts and pastries are what life is all about, right? It's a good thing most Cafés like to display them in all their glory. Just tour the counter and note the name of the sweet treat for you. They are usually conveniently labeled.

Dinner is a smaller meal and can be found in Restaurants or *Lokale* (pubs). Expect dinner to be served from six o'clock until ten o'clock. You should go with self-serve buffets when you can; you know you'll get exactly what you like. The Mövenpick restaurant chain has excellent food throughout Europe.

Once you enter an establishment, don't expect a hostess to seat you, except for at the very finest restaurants. You should just walk in and take a vacant table. Service tends to be slower than in the United States. And don't expect a big smile from the waitress, either. While you are waiting, look at what the other people are eating. Often that is an indication of the best items on the menu. The *Tagesgericht* (daily special) is often a good choice.

YOU'LL THANK YOURSELF LATER

If you learn to recognize only two words in German, they should probably be *Damen* (Women's) and *Herren* (Men's).

German restaurants offer great dishes, such as *Wiener Schnitzel*, (a flattened, battered piece of meat—not the sausage you may be familiar with) and *Sauerbraten*. Many Americans, however, will want to avoid the organ meats on the menu. Waste not want not, or want not waste. Whatever your motto, learn the following dishes and you'll be fine:

> Blutwurst = blood sausage
>
> Leberwurst = liverwurst
>
> Sauer Lungerl = sour lung of veal
>
> Zunge = tongue (Don't knock it until you've tried it. Who knows, it may help get yours around those umlauts!)

When you have finished your meal, don't expect the waiter to whisk away the empty plates. That is considered rude. When you are ready to pay, get out your wallet and flag down the server. You almost always pay the waiter directly after he calculates your tab. German waiters display amazing mathematical talent by adding up your bill on a note pad in front of you. Just look at the number the waiter writes down and round up a bit. Generally, service is included, but you should make the tab come to an even number. If your dinner was 18.30 DM, for example, hand the waiter a 20 DM bill and wave your hand. He'll know the rest is for him.

From Hotel Hopping to Bar Hopping

It's late, you're tired, and you're thinking any inn in a storm. Although the majority of accommodations in the

Congratulations! You have negotiated the train, eaten dinner, and found a hotel. Now go out and treat yourself to a souvenir. A Swiss watch? A beer stein? A Loden coat? You'll be sure to pick up some more German while you shop!

The Lazy Way

Always take a card with your hotel's address when you go out exploring so that you can find it after you've had a few beers and wandered down quaint, twisting alleys. You can always show the card and ask for directions or hand it to a taxi driver if you get lost.

German-speaking world are clean and safe, these tips will give you some ideas on how to spend the night the way you'd like without requiring the night clerk to have studied at Oxford or you to break a sweat pantomiming.

First, you need to realize that budget German accommodations often do not have a private bathroom. Don't be surprised if the toilet is down the hall, along with the shower or bath. This economizing measure saves the owners space and you money. If you don't want to be inconvenienced and don't mind spending a little extra money, ask for a room with a toilet and bath. A sink is often in each room so that you can at least brush your teeth in privacy. You also have the option of selecting *mit Frühstück* (breakfast), *Halbpension* (breakfast and lunch), often abbreviated HP, or *Vollpension* (which includes all three meals), often abbreviated VP.

Have the clerk show you the available rooms and write down the prices so that you know your choices. Take a quick look at the breakfast room, too, to decide if you want to pay extra for a continental breakfast. German breakfast includes coffee or tea, fresh rolls, cheese, sliced sausage, and butter and jam. Extra generous breakfasts include a boiled egg, yogurt, or müsli. Milk and juice are less common choices.

Now you are ready either to tuck in for the night or go out bar hopping. You might as well stay up with your jet lag!

DRESSING THE PART

Most Americans on tour in Europe are easy to spot because of their bright white tennis shoes and more casual style of dress. How do Europeans look so polished all the time? In general, they actually tend to have fewer clothes than the average American, but each piece is of higher quality. Therefore, their basics last forever. And to keep things from getting boring, they are masters of accessories. Fashion-forward scarves, glasses, pins, shoes, and purses are a key part of that "Euro" look. Even men get into the act with playful plastic watches or brightly colored backpacks.

Stylish Europeans would not think of wearing athletic apparel on the street. Leave your tennis shoes at home and invest in some comfortable walking oxfords. They'll help you look the part of a sophisticated traveler.

COUCH KARTOFFEL

Here's homework the way it should be: on the couch and with popcorn! You can watch contemporary films to gain an insight into today's Germany and to improve your language skills.

Your neighborhood video store probably has a few German movies for rent. Almost every store carries Wim Wenders or Rainer Fassbinder movies. You might decide to make a film festival out of it! Pop a bit more corn and invite some friends over to join you on the couch. If you can't find any titles locally, you can always rent movies through the mail from one of the larger movie rental

A COMPLETE WASTE OF TIME

The three worst things you can do when trying to go undercover are:

1. Overdo it with the folk costumes. No one would object to a tasteful *dirndl* (Loden jacket) or maybe a mountaineer's felt hat, but too many local accessories will certainly blow your cover.

2. Use excessive dialect. It's fine to say Grüß Gott instead of Guten Tag when you are in southern Germany, but don't try to mimic the local dialect. Some things are best learned on mother's lap.

3. Disrupt church services with talking, flash photography, or gawking. Many tourists forget that churches are places of worship and not museums. Be considerate while you enjoy the architecture and solace.

houses that specialize in foreign films, such as Chicago-based, non-profit Facets Video. Call them at 1-800-532-2387 or check out their Web site at www.facets.org. They'll mail you a tape or DVD, and you mail it back when you are done. (Don't forget to rewind the tape!) What could be lazier?

Here are some titles to get you started:

- *Jenseits der Stille* (**Beyond Silence**): A story of a hearing girl with two deaf parents.

- *Das Leben ist eine Baustelle* (**Life is a Construction Zone**): A love story, starring great actors, set in Berlin of the 90s.

- *Lola rennt* (**Lola Runs**): A modern classic set in Berlin, captures the 90s.

- *Der Totmacher*: A portrait of a child killer in the 1920s, based on the notes of a court psychologist.

- *Rossini*: A comedy about a bar frequented by the rich and beautiful of Munich.

- *Der bewegte Mann*: A film version of a popular gay comic strip.

- *Das Kondom des Grauens*: A tongue-in-cheek mystery about a killer condom running amok; also based on a popular gay comic book.

- *Knocking on Heaven's Door*: A German road movie with the handsome young star Till Schweiger.

- *Comedian Harmonists*: A film about a popular a cappella group in the 20s and 30s that was prohibited by the Nazis.

QUICK ☜☞ PAINLESS

You'll notice that Germans have different noises of astonishment than Americans. If you are really impressed with something, instead of saying "wow," say "buwah!" Or if you bump your lip with an overly energetic swing of the beer stein, say "auwa" instead of "ouch." You'll sound just like a native.

Regardless of your taste in movies, you can find something in German to enjoy. Although German films have the reputation of being oh-so serious, modern directors are causing quite a buzz with great comedies. And if you see a movie while you are in Germany, don't be surprised by the beer for sale at the snack bar.

IF YOU'RE SO
INCLINED

German almost became the national language of the United States. In fact, Benjamin Franklin favored making it our national language. Many cities in the United States had daily newspapers in German, and some still do. Today, more than 60 percent of Americans claim German as part of their heritage. Still, during World War II, words like Sauerkraut and Kindergarten were Americanized. ("Liberty Cabbage" doesn't sound as yummy as Sauerkraut, does it?)

If You Can't Join 'Em, Beat 'Em: Circumventing the System

Sometimes it is better to cheat—or admit you need help. You can save precious time and money by finding creative work-arounds to actually having to learn German yourself. This chapter will show you shortcuts and sneaky tricks that work in even the wurst-case scenarios.

GAIN WITHOUT THE PAIN

You can break through the language barrier various ways without breaking out in a sweat. Basically, you can capitulate and communicate in English, or delegate and let someone else speak German for you. Each of these strategies has pros and cons. Regardless which you choose, I'll show you the most painless way to get your point across.

Go with What You Know

As an English speaker, you are lucky. English is one of the most widely spoken second languages in the world. You can always just ask politely, in English, whether someone speaks English. Chances are someone will be able to help you. Swiss, Austrians and most Germans educated in the Western part of the country after World War II have had several years of English in high school. In fact, you can turn this into a flattering strategy by complementing your conversation partner on his masterful command of English. Sometimes you can actually get better service by letting the clerk show off a bit in English than by insisting he limp along with your German.

You can also recruit hapless bystanders into helping you communicate. If the person you are trying to speak with doesn't understand English, chances are that someone else close by does. Politely press them into service and thank them for their help. Maybe you'll be able to return the favor someday.

If English fails, find out if you have another language in common. The Swiss, for example, are likely to speak French and Italian in addition to German; Eastern Germans probably studied Russian.

Remember that communicating with someone in their second or even third language can easily result in misunderstandings. If something doesn't make sense or seems entirely ridiculous (such as, "Flight tool boarding at gate 22"), get a second opinion.

Second Languages

The English that Germans learn in school is British English. Americanisms will be unfamiliar to most people. You will be better understood if you speak slowly and avoid slang expressions. Contrary to popular belief, however, you don't need to yell when communicating with foreigners!

When you are speaking English with German speakers, there are some things you can do to improve your communication situation.

QUICK ⬤ PAINLESS

Politely ask the German-speaking person behind the counter if he or she speaks English.

- **Smile, make a joke, or find some way to break the ice:** Put your partner at ease. American films are popular in Europe; try mentioning one of them.

- **Complement their English:** Most people know more English than they think they do. If you encourage them to shine, they often will.

- **Start the ball rolling with an easy question:** You can get to the trick questions once you have established common ground.

- **Remember to be patient:** A moment of silence might just mean your informant is thinking.

- **Repeat your conversation partner's responses:** It will make them feel good to know you are following them, and you'll be showing interest in what they have to say.

- **Don't correct their English in front of others:** Nothing will stop a conversation faster in its tracks than a grammar school teacher reflex to correct every little mistake your partner makes.

Phrase Books Without the Frazzle

Tourists have relied on phrase books for centuries. Despite their obvious limitations in achieving flexibility or pronunciation, they can come in handy. You don't even have to open your mouth; you can often just point at the phrase you need to communicate. Have your partner point to the response. (Note that well-manicured fingers are highlighted with this method of communication. Ladies, paint yours in compelling carmine to guide your reader to the target faster.)

You can also make a cheat sheet of phrases you know you'll need and carry it with you. By the time you need them, however, you probably will have already learned them. If you want an extra security blanket, go ahead and bring it along. Communication is an open-book test!

Admit You Need Help—Hiring a Pro

Delegation is a great thing. The world is complex; you can't know everything. Sometimes it is a good idea to let somebody else do the job. You'll pay a price for the service, of course. In some situations, however, such as business or research, it often makes sense either to hire a professional translator to bridge the language barrier, or to bring an interpreter to an important meeting.

Language professionals, such as interpreters and translators, train with post-graduate studies to leap with agility across language barriers. You can find them by looking under "Translators" in the Yellow Pages. More and more translators and translation companies are working for clients over the Internet. (See the list of

A COMPLETE WASTE OF TIME

The three worst things you can do to make your foreign language experience stressful:

1. Be proud. You have to be willing to make mistakes to learn. It's time to be humble.

2. Be shy. Speak up and go with the flow; you'll blend right in.

3. Lose your cool. Don't ever be embarrassed that you can't speak German as well as you'd like. Sometimes you can just say, "Guten Tag! Sprechen Sie Englisch?" and continue your inquiry in English.

sources in Appendix A, "How to Get Someone Else to Do It.") Think of it like hiring a contractor to remodel your bathroom rather than doing it yourself. Sometimes you just want things done professionally (not a bad idea when it comes to plumbing or business negotiations).

You'll notice that many translation agencies specialize in certain languages and subjects. The end result often will be better and cheaper if you can find an agency that specifically works in German and English and that also understands your subject matter. Note that there is a difference between an interpreter and a translator. A *translator* works with written texts, whereas an *interpreter* works with clients in "live" situations. Some professionals are skilled in both, but most do only one or the other.

When interviewing a potential language professional, you should ask the following questions:

- **What is the translator's native language?** Professional translators work only into their native language from their foreign language. This ensures a greater degree of quality.

- **Does the translator work with an editor?** Two sets of eyes are always better than one. Professional documents should be reviewed by a team, just like you would always want someone to proofread an important English text.

- **Is the translator a member of the American Translator's Association or another professional group?** Members of professional associations take their work seriously, strive to provide quality

A COMPLETE WASTE OF TIME

When learning German you have to be tough. Avoid these pitfalls:

1. Expecting Germans speakers to want to speak English with you.

2. Succumbing to the temptation to speak only English. Go ahead and use German where you can.

3. Being a perfectionist. Be willing to make mistakes. Learn by leaping!

translations, and participate in continuing education courses.

- **How is the price determined for the job?** Does the price include desktop publishing and layout services? Who pays the interpreter's travel expenses? An agency should give you a binding quote for a particular job. You should have them look at the text, and inform them whether it's for publication (which requires the highest standards for copy writing) and what output you want; for example, should they send the translation by e-mail, fax, or the mail? Prices vary and so does quality. A good translation may cost a bit more, but it will likely be worth it. Misunderstandings can be very expensive in the long run. Insist on a written contract so that you know which services are covered.

- **Does the translator have references?** How long has she been translating? What was her professional training? A good education in translation, a proven track record, and happy customers are always good, common-sense proof of a professional's abilities.

Insider's Guide to Interpreting

So you've decided to hire a professional interpreter for that big presentation to your German account. So far, so good. If you have never worked with an interpreter, there are a few things you'll want to know before you jump up on center stage.

The following are the two basic types of interpretation:

- **Simultaneous:** This method uses headsets to broadcast the interpretation to the audience in multiple languages. This method commonly is used in the United Nations or large conferences where you see everyone wearing headsets. Some summarization is necessary to keep pace with the original. Expect to get about 90 percent of the content converted for your audience.

- **Consecutive:** This method requires the interpreter to listen to about three minutes of the original and then have the speaker pause for the interpretation. This method is used in most business settings and court proceedings. One of the greatest advantages to using an interpreter is that the time it takes for the translation buys you time to consider a deal or offer a negotiation.

Whichever method you use, it will greatly benefit the interpreter if you can supply her with a copy of your notes, speech, or other background material before the presentation, so that she can prepare for the terminology and special aspects of your text.

Internationalize It First!

Before you attempt to cross a language barrier, you should first think about what parts of your message could be lost in the translation. Some typical examples are things like puns that do not translate well, baseball

QUICK ◖**ɪɪ**◗ *PAINLESS*

When working with an interpreter, remember to slow down your pace and avoid culture-specific humor and puns. The interpreter will thank you, and your audience will get a clearer translation of your message.

Regardless of the language your message is in, you can give it a German look with the right typeface. Treat your word processor to a well-designed German typeface to give everything you write that German flair. For an old-fashioned look, you may want to use a Fraktur typeface; or maybe you prefer the clean lines of the Bauhaus design. Visit www.adobe.com for free samples.

analogies, or culturally specific humor. Although substitute humor can be found, the effect will certainly be different. Also remember that Europe uses the metric system; you will want to convert accordingly.

TAKE A BYTE OUT OF IT

When the supercomputer Big Blue recently won a chess match against world champion Garry Kasparov, it was heralded as a major victory for computer science. As a result, many of my clients asked me if computers would soon be putting human translators out of business. Although many millions of dollars have been spent researching and developing machine translation, sci-fi translator machines are still a distant dream. There are so many variables, so many nuances, and so many things that depend on context and associations that machines just can't get right without human help. Unfortunately, you can't spend $29.95 and get a software program that accurately translates texts with the click of a button. Sure, there are companies out there that will sell them to you, but there are also companies that will sell you exercise contraptions and convince you that you can look like Arnold Schwarzenegger in just 30 days. Remember: If it sounds too good to be true, it probably is!

The easiest way to find out if these programs can help you is to try them yourself. You can try one for free at Alta Vista's Web site (http://babelfish.altavista.digital. com/cgi-bin/translate?). You'll soon discover the program's limitations, but sometimes a translator in the hand is better than two in the bush. You can use it to at least get a rough idea about what the text might be about.

Here's an example of the program's handiwork:

Hi Andreas. We'll come visit you in Berlin on March 21.

This was translated into:

Hallo Andreas. Wir kommen Besuch Sie in Berlin an März 21.

This translation is understandable nonsense. The proper translation is:

Hallo Andreas. Wir besuchen Dich am 21. März in Berlin.

Or look at this gem:

Liebe Amy,

Wir kommen zu Besuch am 21. März.

Bis dann!

Andreas

This was translated into:

Dear Amy, we comes to the attendance on 21 March. Until then! Andreas

As you can see, although this program is limited in its ability, you can sort of guess at the meaning of the translation. You can also see, however, how it could cause misunderstandings.

In fact, you should always double-check important documents with a human translator. You should also preface any document translated by machine with a

Many tours of castles, cities, or museums are periodically offered in English. Ask when the next tour in English is available. If you have to wait a bit, enjoy the view or rest your tired feet in a cozy café until it's time to get started.

The Lazy Way

disclaimer stating that the document was translated by a software program. You may also want to attach an English version of the text so that your reader can refer to it, as necessary. (For other resources, see Appendix A, "How to Get Someone Else to Do It.")

PRACTICAL PRACTICE: PLANNING YOUR DREAM TRIP

Even if you are heading to the German-speaking world, there will be time for a detour or two to the Alps, a castle on the Rhine, the opera, or a museum at one of the famous German car manufacturers. (And regardless whether you are actually going to Europe or not, you can always have fun dreaming.) You can get materials to help plan your trip from the Tourist Bureaus of Austria, Germany, and Switzerland, as well as of individual cities. A large amount of information is available on the Internet just for the clicking. Your local library will also have travel videos, books, and magazines to inspire you.

Sprachvergnügen: How to Make It All Stick

How do you learn a language? Practice, practice, practice, right? Well, mostly. But how should you practice? What does the mind need to do to learn and later retain language as efficiently as possible? This chapter will first look at the mechanics of memory and then make sure you have enough ideas about how to have fun while you are practicing.

You've heard Volkswagen's ad campaign capitalizing on *Fahrvergnügen*—literally, "driving" (*fahren*) "pleasure" (*Vergnügen*)." Well, Sprachvergnügen is our motto, and it means "language pleasure."

Of course, you want to make your practice sessions as pleasurable as possible. I'll even venture to say that later you will want to retain all you've learned in the easiest and most pleasant way possible. No worries. This chapter outlines fun and lazy ways to acquire language skills and then gives you tips on how to keep your skills sharp, such as by watching movies, getting together with friends, or listening to music. So

that you don't get bored, I'll show you some fun ways to integrate speaking German into your everyday life; studying will become so second nature that you won't even know you are doing it.

Bau the Haus—Building a Foundation

How does the brain store information? Building a vocabulary is very much like building a house; it goes up brick by brick. The key is finding strong, durable mortar to hold the bricks of words together so that they will be there when you need them. Once you understand how the mind links unknown concepts to known concepts, the process is simplified. This understanding allows you to make the most of the various types of memory. And naturally, without a reason to learn something, the mind wanders. Knowing these basic principles makes it easier for you to learn faster.

Associations—Apply Here

You can accelerate your retention of new concepts by actively looking for associations to familiar concepts. The classic "mnemonic" method serves as a bridge between the known and the unknown. It also has a second function of forcing you to actively pay attention to the word. As you search for a useful mnemonic xxx, you will undoubtedly spend time pondering the word, which will also familiarize your mind with the term.

Here's an example. The German word for egg is *das Ei*. What unique characteristics does the word have?

1. It is pronounced almost exactly like the English word "eye" or "I."

2. It is also a two-letter word, which makes it stand out in the German Forest of Long Words.

3. Both letters are vowels.

4. It starts with *E* just like "egg" does in English. (I am sure if you look harder you will find some associations of your own.)

The trick is to come up with a way to use these associations to link the unknown, the German word for egg, to a familiar memorable image. If you find a vivid enough picture, you will never forget the word. (Even if I call you at three o'clock in the morning to ask you, "Quick, how do you say egg in German?" you will be able to answer without thinking.)

There are innumerable ways to do so, and I suggest that you try your hand at it. Here are some ideas to get you started:

1. Picture a hard-boiled egg with big eyelashes. The eye is *das Ei*.

2. Imagine yourself saying, "I have egg on my face." The egg is directly linked to the word "I," which sounds like *das Ei*.

3. Instead of a little dot on top of the *i* in *Ei*, picture an Easter egg.

When learning additional words, you'll need to come up with your own tricks. Remember to take your learning style (which we determined back in Chapter 1) into account. See, the knowledge you are gaining in this book is building on itself like a little gabled brick house.

IF YOU'RE SO *INCLINED*

Want more real-life language piped directly into your living room? You can travel the world with the transistor! Check out short-wave radio. Put up your rabbit ears and tune it in.

The Long and the Short of It

Short-term and long-term memory are familiar phrases and concepts. However, things aren't quite that simple. Human memories are now commonly thought to be made up of three different types of memory. From briefest to longest, they are: working memory, holding memory, and permanent memory.

Working memory usually lasts no longer than a half a minute or so and is rather limited in capacity. It is useful for repeating back unfamiliar information, such as a new word or a person's name. The information will be gone quickly unless you lock it in by transferring it to holding memory.

Holding memory lasts more than half a minute but not long enough to be permanent. This is the most vulnerable category because the data can easily be lost before it is permanently warehoused.

Permanent memory includes the securely filed items that will be there when you look for them. The goal is to move the loose data from holding memory into permanent memory as quickly as possible.

One key to moving information from one category to another is repetition or practice. Breaking up practice sessions and revisiting topics after a pause of several hours encourages the migration into permanent storage. Even just a quick review of your vocabulary written into your day planner or a list taped to the fridge can serve this purpose. My teacher of Ancient Greek once told me that I would remember forever anything I wrote down nine times. He was almost right. I remembered it for the

IF YOU'RE SO INCLINED

The study of language and memory is fascinating reading. For an advanced discussion of these principles and the latest research, you may want to read *Memory, Meaning and Method: A View of Language Teaching,* by Earl W. Stevick.

next test. Don't ask me to remember it right now! I have lost my reason for doing so, because seldom do I need to read Homer in my everyday life. You, on the other hand, will have many reasons to keep up with your German. Right?

Learning Under Pressure

Speaking of tests, you may be surprised to know that learning also requires a certain amount of healthy stress. Studies have shown that some pressure, such as an upcoming exam or presentation, actually encourages the brain to remember. Before you sign up for the college-level German tests hoping to light a fire under your desk chair, however, note that although some pressure is good, too much will shut down your receptiveness to learning. (Another example of how all things are best in moderation.)

GET SOME CLASS—FINDING A LEARNING SITUATION

Even independent students need a classy learning environment and supplies. Spoil yourself by spending the time and energy to make your learning experience the best it can be. You can make it easier to learn if you work in a quiet space with your dictionary, flash cards, and note paper close at hand. The space can be at a desk or in your favorite easy chair. You can motivate yourself by posting a few pictures or postcards near your work that remind you of why you want to learn German. And if you want to join a group or find a private tutor, here are pointers to lock in on the right situation for you.

QUICK PAINLESS

Are you a TV junkie? When traveling, you can take a stab at understanding German television. Whereas some programs may be difficult, the commercials are short and offer a great repetitive opportunity to practice pronunciation. Just listen and repeat the latest pitch for diet cola or laundry soap.

Make It a Social Event

Some people find learning with others a big motivation. Here are some ideas to turn your German learning experience into a social success. (You might meet a travel partner or get a few tips on the best Bed & Breakfast in Berlin, too!)

Many communities have clubs for German speakers. They may present guest speakers or just meet once a month to gab and eat at a *Stammtisch* (a table for regulars) at a local restaurant. Ask around and see whether there is a group that interests you.

You might also find that your local community college, adult night school, or Goethe Institute offers German conversation courses. Sign up for one and meet others with similar interests. If you can't find time to take a regular class, you may want to engage a tutor to meet with you at your convenience. Tutors are not very expensive, and the individual attention and flexibility can be a big advantage. Look for someone who has tutored before and has enthusiasm for the subject.

Big-city folks may find a course that fits their schedule at the Goethe Institute. Most major cities in the United States have one. These institutes are located around the world and work on behalf of the German government to provide German cultural and language educational programs to the public. They also offer courses in Germany and certification exams in German. Call 212-439-8700 to contact the Goethe Institut in New York City to find the one nearest you, or check out their Web site (www.goethe.de).

Regardless of the class you take, consider the following factors:

1. How often does the group meet? Once a week is a bare minimum.

2. How many students are in the class? The fewer the better.

3. What level are the other students? It is often better to be the worst in a group than the best. You can always learn from the others.

4. Are the time and location convenient for you? The easier it is to get there, the less likely you'll find an excuse to miss class.

5. Can you meet the instructor and see if you click? You have to like a teacher to learn from them. (Unlike in junior high, you are taking this class by choice!)

LEARNING TO BE AN ARMCHAIR LEARNER

I like to compare speaking a foreign language to athletic training. There are a lot of different levels of runners, for example, and a lot of different levels of German speakers. Some people may jog once a month and never want to run a triathlon. Some people may need a few phrases for a vacation and never want to have a long conversation or write a business letter in German. The good thing is that whatever your goal, you can master German from your armchair—which is much more comfortable than training for most sporting events.

IF YOU'RE SO
INCLINED

Double your pleasure. Make a list in German for chores you regularly do around the house: *Küche* (kitchen), *Müll* (trash), *Staubsauger* (vacuum), *Wäsche* (laundry), and so on. Use this list to keep track of jobs, and you'll soon know how to say them in German.

As a professional German-language translator and consultant, I consider myself to be the equivalent of a professional triathlete in German. I have to read, write, and speak on a professional level. Of course, I didn't acquire these skills by sitting on the couch, just like I couldn't run the Iron Man off the couch either! To get where I am, I had to practice, practice, practice. And I still have to train every day. (Think about those old guys who talk about their glory days out on the old college field; if they had to run today, they would sure huff around the quarter mile. The same thing happens to your language: If you don't use it, you lose it!)

Naturally, I want to keep up with my German in the most pleasurable way possible. To make my training fun, I try to vary my workouts. I read a magazine, watch a movie, meet with friends, or surf the Web. I also research new topics that interest me to expand my active knowledge. You should do the same if you want to get your German in shape.

Don't be too hard on yourself if you can't run a marathon the first day on the track. You will work up to it. And don't get down if you used to speak great German. You will again. You can't expect to run a four-minute mile off the couch! And, as in sports, it is the consistent effort that pays off, not the cramming crunches. It is better to set a realistic goal and work towards it at a reasonable pace than to get disappointed when your German isn't pumping up like Hans and Franz on steroids. With that said, let the games begin!

IF YOU'RE SO
INCLINED

Like to spend time on the Internet? Visit one of the many newsgroups for a discussion in German. AOL and other providers also offer online chat in German. You don't even have to participate. Following simple conversations will improve your skills.

TECHNIKEN, TIPS, AND TRICKS FOR LEARNING ON YOUR OWN

Ready for the ultimate learning experience? Language immersion doesn't mean you have to get wet. Easy ways to immerse yourself include movies, restaurants, the Internet, tapes, and talking to yourself and your pets. The best way to get yourself to practice is to make it a fun part of your lifestyle. The following exercise suggestions provide examples of the many ways you can integrate speaking German into your busy life without taking any extra time.

German Combos

Food and language learning go together like sausage and sauerkraut. Take advantage of it! Many cities in the United States are fortunate to have German bakeries. Visit one and ask for some specialties of the house and their German names. You can eat and learn at the same time. Some of my favorites include: *Bienenstich* (literally, a bee sting), a layered yeast cake filled with cream and topped with caramelized almonds, or the classic *Brezel* (a big, soft pretzel). You really can't go wrong.

Talk to Your German Equipment in German

You can post notes on your household items to label them in German. It's a fun way to greet your *Spiegel* (mirror) every morning or your *Kaffeemaschine* (coffee maker) while you learn some new German vocabulary.

Perhaps you have a German sports car (or pretend you do). Sometimes it is fun to memorize a few lines to

IF YOU'RE SO
INCLINED

The next chance you get, casually mention at the office or club that you are learning German in order to take a performance driving course in the Alps next summer; be the lead baritone/bass/alto/soprano in the Met's production of *Tristan und Isolde*; or to better understand the temporal nuances (as expressed in the original German) of Einstein's theories of relativity. You'll earn respect.

It's easy to incorporate a few German curses into your day. Here are some that aren't too offensive but that will get the matter of your displeasure across:

Dummkopf or *Dummköpfe* (Dumbhead or dummy)

Sie dummer Pinsel! (You dumb paintbrush—for men)

Mist! (Manure—a classic expletive in German that is also safe around children)

use every time you start it. When it performs well, you should praise it in German. Make it a habit to use the following phrases when talking to your car:

Du bist so ein tolles Auto! (You are such a great car!)

Fahren wir? (Shall we drive?)

Ich liebe 300 PS! (I love 300 horsepower!)

Schneller! (Faster!)

Keine Angst! (Do not be afraid!)

Geben Sie mir acht Zylinder oder geben Sie mir den Tod! (Give me eight cylinders or give me death!)

Unsere Fahrt war wirklich aufregend. (Our drive was truly thrilling.)

Dieses Geheimnis bleibt zwischen uns. (This secret will stay between us.)

Learn some standard phrases that you can use over and over again in different situations. You can be creative and sound eloquent with just a few clever twists of the tongue. You can take some cues from the following fantasy dialogs.

You may have slick German bathroom fixtures (if not, you may pretend). Ask them nicely in German if they would like to serve you:

Würden Sie mich bitte bedienen? (Would you please serve me?)

Ich möchte heisses (kaltes) Wasser. (I want hot [cold] water.)

Sie sind so modern! (You are so modern!)

Darf ich Sie fotographieren? (May I photograph you?)

You can also learn some useful lines by practicing with your pen. Tell your precision German writing instrument that it is your favorite, and you will never lose it:

Mein Lieber, Du bist mein Liebling! Ich werde Dich nie verlieren! Ich drücke Dich ganz fest an mein Herz. Ich werde Dich auf immer und ewig in meiner Tasche tragen. (My dear, you are my favorite. I will never lose you! You will stay very close to my heart. I will keep you in my pocket for ever and ever.)

You may also want to address your imported beer in German:

Prost! (Cheers!)

Das ist wirklich eine Spezialität! (That is truly a specialty!)

Es schmeck sehr gut. (It tastes very good.)

Noch eine Runde? (Another round?)

Klar! (Certainly!)

Talk to Everyone You Can in German

You should try to speak as much German as possible. Learn to look for situations in which you can practice. Here are some ideas to get you started.

Find someone who wants to learn German and practice together. You could go see a foreign film or go for a German dinner. Most importantly, you should speak

Notice that German is a graphic language, which makes many words deceptively easy to learn and often riotously funny, as well. Pull these out at your next office party or social gathering:

Staubsauger (dust + sucker = vacuum cleaner)

Schleimhaut (slime + skin = mucous membrane)

Fußpilz (foot + mushroom = athlete's foot)

German with that person. (You could also find a native German speaker who wants to work on her English, and work out a trade.) Put an ad in a local newspaper and see who responds.

If you want to impress the respondents to your ad, you may want to try recording your answering machine message in German. A sample text:

Danke für Ihren Anruf. Bitte hinterlassen Sie eine Nachricht nach dem Signalton. (Thank you for your call. Please leave a message after the beep.)

Modern technology has made it painless to reach around the world. *Surfen Sie das Web!* Spend some time on the Internet looking for German-language sites that interest you. These may be newspapers or hobby- or business-related sites. Let your browser take you to some German. See the list of Web resources in Appendix B, "If You Really Want More." You can also use the Internet to find a pen pal. Who knows, you may even want to visit him or her on your next trip to Europe! Check out www.penpal.net for free introductions.

Talk to Yourself in German

If you can't find anyone or anything to talk to, you can always talk to yourself. Maybe this should not be done out loud, though, okay?

One idea is to make out your next shopping list in German. Then, while you are in the grocery store, think through your list and use it while thinking in German.

For extra practice with numbers, read the prices in German!

If you are more romantically inclined, memorize a poem or song in German for a loved one. Memorizing a short verse will not be only a great party trick, it will help you increase your memory skills, vocabulary, and grammar.

Or, if you prefer the international language of music, let some music take you away. See the list at the end of Chapter 1, "Stranger in a Strange Language: What You Should Know Before We Start." Whatever your musical tastes, you will find a way to indulge them in German—from rap to opera to folk music.

Speaking of the arts, are you the next Kafka? Keep your journal in German. You might just try to record one thing in German, such as the weather. The idea is to write something in German every day. You'll be able to look back at it and see the metamorphosis!

THE NAME GAME

Johann Wolfgang von Goethe (1749–1832) [say GEWta] is one of the most famous writers in German literature and a key figure in the age of enlightenment. (His is probably also the most mispronounced name by English speakers. Remember: The *h* is silent in German.) A master of poetry, drama, and the novel, his most famous work is the dramatic two-part poem *Faust*. If you travel to Weimar, you can visit his final home. Frankfurt has made his childhood home into a beautiful museum.

QUICK PAINLESS

Read German literature in translation. It might motivate you to get your German good enough to read it in the original. Top choices include: poems by Goethe or Rilke; *The Magic Mountain,* by Thomas Mann; *The Metamorphosis,* by Franz Kafka; *Steppenwolf,* by Hermann Hesse; and *Perfume,* by Patrick Süskind.

Exercise 1

Using the name Johann Wolfgang von Goethe, see how many German words you can create:

Tag (day)

Tee (tea)

_____

_____

_____

_____

_____

Now see how many other words you can find in long famous German names. It will be easy compared to having to sign those long names!

Sie Sprechen Deutsch?

Are You Too Lazy to Read Sie Sprechen Deutsch?

1 There is a good chance you could eventually get sick of eating only Apfelstrudel for breakfast, lunch, and dinner. ☐ yes ☐ no

2 You can translate "Der Ring ist gold" without reaching for a dictionary. ☐ yes ☐ no

3 Correspondence? That's something best left to the news media! ☐ yes ☐ no

Cognates: Old Friends in New Clothes

Welcome to the wonderful world of cognates—the words you easily recognize because you already know their English cousins. It's a wonderful world, right? And, in many ways, a small world. That's why some German sentences will be obvious to English speakers; for example: *Der Wolf hat Hunger im Winter*. What could be lazier?

COMMON CAUSES, COMMON WORDS

A little knowledge of the history of a language can really help you increase your vocabulary and "decoding" skills when you face an unknown word. History progresses, and it should be no surprise that back in the early part of the millennium, the languages that became today's English and German shared the same words for things like gold, wolf, and winter—just like today they use the same words for computers, sex, and jeans. Folks are folks with the same interests and concerns then and now. You'll see just how much we have in common with our German-speaking cousins and learn some nifty tools to "uncover" lost, related words.

ENGLISH AND GERMAN ARE OLD FRIENDS

Imagine Europe 1,500 years ago. What languages were being spoken? And how do we know? Not too many people were writing or reading back then, so what we do know comes primarily from church documents and fragments of famous tales and poems that started to appear about 1,000 years ago. You won't be surprised to learn that some of the first written examples of German were actually early phrase books for traveling clergy! (An example of one of these phrases is: "Why weren't you at Matins?")

And that leads to a discussion of the two predominant language families in Europe: Romance and Germanic, both of which are members of the larger Indo-European language family.

Romance languages have their roots in Latin. The influence of Latin spread across Europe to form the basis for the Romance languages such as French, Spanish, and Italian. Numerous dialects were spoken by the geographically isolated groups of Germanic tribes north of the Alps. We call those languages "Germanic" or "Teutonic." (See how "Teutonic" looks almost like *Deutsch*? You'll understand the similarities once I explain the code a little later in this chapter.)

The family of Germanic languages has evolved to include modern-day Danish, Dutch (which went on to

Learn to recognize cognates whenever you can. The German words for hand, gold, finger, bitter, and arm are the same as in English, for example.

The Lazy Way

become the basis for Afrikaans in South Africa), Swedish, Icelandic, Norwegian, Yiddish (which is written with Hebrew characters but based on many German words), and, most importantly for you, German and English. Just look at the long list of languages you will know more about when you finish this lesson!

THE GOOD NEWS

This may come as a surprise, but as a speaker of English you have already mastered a Germanic language! That's the good news. And there's more good news: All Germanic languages have a common history and, thus, common words (called *cognates*). Like a long-lost cousin might have the same famous family nose or ears that you recognize from looking in the mirror, these cousin languages share traits and roots that you will recognize. These are great shortcuts for the lazy learner, because you don't have to learn anything. These are words or roots you already know. And it is not surprising that these words refer to the most basic things in life. If you are stuck looking for the right word, it may be easier to find than you think.

As time goes on languages add their own new words. The new words are influenced by other sources, so don't expect every word to explain itself directly from our common heritage. However, a large number of words have common roots. Let's look at some of the most easy to recognize first.

A COMPLETE WASTE OF TIME

Some tips regarding learning German versus other Germanic languages...

1. Don't think that if you speak Swedish or Dutch that you'll automatically be able to understand German.

2. Don't neglect to benefit from the cognates in other Germanic languages you may know, including English.

3. Don't expect to find all cognates served to you on a platter. Some cognates are hidden under slight modifications.

Remember that not all German words that look like English words are cognates. Some apparent allies are really false friends. The German word *die*, for example, is not "dead;" it is the feminine definite article. And the German word *hat* is not "a head covering;" it means "has."

Full Cognates

The following is a list of full cognates in German and English. These words are exactly the same in English and in German. How much easier could it be to recognize the meanings? Note how they refer to basic necessities for primitive communication, including body parts, objects, and descriptive expressions.

English	German
Arm	*der Arm*
Finger	*der Finger*
Hand	*die Hand*
Gold	*das Gold*
Hammer	*der Hammer*
Ring	*der Ring*
Rose	*die Rose*
Sack	*das Sack*
Winter	*der Winter*
Wolf	*der Wolf*
Bitter	*bitter*
Mild	*mild*
Warm	*warm*

Isn't this great? You're already able to communicate all those basic, primal needs you have in common with our distant ancestors who lived almost 2,000 years ago!

THE BAD NEWS

The bad news is that as time went on, things changed. Actually, that isn't all that bad. What changed? Well, the sounds did. And thanks to Jakob Grimm (whose name you will recognize as the collector of those grim and fanciful *Grimm's Fairy Tales*), there are rules that explain what happened. Grimm called the phenomenon he observed the "sound shift;" it is now known as Grimm's Law. It shows the difference between Low German (like Anglo-Saxon) and High German—which explains why Germans call pennies *Pfennige*, and why *Zehn* sounds like "ten," among other things.

For you, the consequences of this historic discovery help uncover disguised common words in English and German. Although these words aren't quite as easy to remember as the full cognates listed earlier in this chapter, they certainly will be useful tools in your lazy way war chest. Consider them to be your magic decoder rings; they will often help you decipher a word you may not otherwise recognize.

How the Decoding System Works

The following rules show how to uncover the common words in German and English that grew apart over time. Look at the German word and apply the following "code" to it, and you will see an English word emerge. It's like magic!

YOU'LL THANK YOURSELF LATER

When learning nouns, make sure to learn them along with their articles (for example, *der*, *die*, or *das*). Remember that articles indicate whether a noun is masculine (*der*), feminine (*die*), or neuter (*das*). It is best to learn a noun's gender as you go, because a noun's gender is really an integral part of German words.

The rules for consonants are:

German consonant becomes English consonant	Example
b > b (initial position)	*best* > best
b (middle position) *> v*	*das Silber* > silver
b (final position) *> f*	*halb* > half
ch > k	*die Milch* > milk
cht >ght	*recht* > right
d > th	*das Bad* > bath, *das Ding* > thing
f > p (middle or final position)	*helfen* > help, *reif* > ripe
g > y	*das Garn* > yarn
k > ch	*das Kinn* > chin
mm > mb	*dumm* > dumb
n > drop *n*	*der Stern* > star
pf > p or *pp*	*der Apfel* > apple
s or *ss > t*	*das Wasser* > water
t > d	*der Gott* > god
v > f	*der Vater* > father
z > t	*zwei* > two

The rules for vowels are:

German vowel becomes English vowel	Example
a > o	*lang* > long
a > ae	*klar* > clear

IF YOU'RE SO
INCLINED

Even today's dialects in Germany are evident of the differences between German and English. Speakers in northern Germany say, *Ik, Maken and Appel* instead of *Ich, Machen and Apfel*. Doesn't the former sound a lot like the English words "I," "make," and "apple?"

au > ou	das Haus > house
e > i	recht > right
ie > ee	das Bier > beer
u > oo	das Buch > book
u >ou	der Grund > ground

Look at what these few rules can let you decode. The lazy possibilities are really great!

Exercise 1

Here's a sample story you should easily understand by applying your "code." Try to read through the text and "uncover" the cognates to discover the meaning of this little story.

Ich habe ein altes Hausboot. Es ist Sommer. Vater und Onkel bringen Wein und Bier. Es ist eine heisse Nacht. Mein Bett ist sanft. Wir schlafen. Die Tuer ist offen. Ein Dieb kommt. Der Dieb will mein Silber. Der Mond scheint. Er sieht Silber. Er ist dumm. Er hat meinen Fisch!

_____

—

_____

—

_____

—

_____

—

Visual learners would benefit from designing a decoder ring for German and English consonants and vowel equivalents. What would yours look like?

The Lazy Way

—

After you have worked through the text, compare your answer with the answer key in Appendix D. How close did you get? Do you see how it helps to be lazy and learn a few simple rules rather than a long list of vocabulary?

Exercise 2

Here's another exercise for you. Deduce the meanings of the following phrases using the code you now know. (Drop the underlined endings to make it easy.)

Tief<u>es</u> Wasser   _____

Kalt<u>es</u> Fleisch   _____

Gut<u>en</u> Tag!   _____

Apfelkuchen   _____

ALMOST FRIENDS AND FALSE FRIENDS

Over time, of course, some German and English cognates have developed different meanings. Usually, these meanings are just wrong enough to get you into trouble if used as literal translations; thus, caution is in order. Think of them as *almost friends*. Nonetheless, they often can help you decipher meanings because they are still related (albeit somewhat distantly) in meaning. In these cases, it makes sense to refer to a dictionary for the actual meaning. Also note that these cognates can help you remember a German word by serving as a mnemonic device.

German	English cognate	English meaning
das Bein	bone	leg
die Blume	bloom	flower
sterben	to starve	to die
fahren	to fare	to travel
streng	strong	strict

A word of caution: Some German words may coincidentally look like English words but have totally different meanings. These words are called *false friends*. (You knew this sounded too easy.) So, if you are working through a text and find something that just does not sound right, reach for a dictionary and check it out. It may be one of these false friends:

Bekommen (to receive)

das Gift (poison)

die (the)

rot (red)

You can see how, if mistaken, these could get you into trouble!

Das ist trendy!

A long list of English words has also been "adopted" into

QUICK ⬤ PAINLESS

Even false friends can be useful. Use the image of the English cognate to help you remember the translation. The meaning is often related, as in *das Fleisch* (meat); "flesh" is the cognate, which is related to the meaning, "meat."

QUICK ■ PAINLESS

German. These are mostly words for things in our modern culture or inventions from America. The list includes:

comic strip (*der Comic*)

computer (*der Computer*)

defroster (*der Defroster*)

jazz (*der Jazz*)

jersey (*der Jersey*)

job (*der Job*)

sex (*der Sex*)

jean (*die Jeans*)

Note that all of these words are masculine in German. Most borrowed words from English are. "Jeans" is plural, so they are *die Jeans* in German.

Exercise 3

See how much you can understand of the following little text written in German and spiked with borrowed words from English, and then write your translation:

Ich bin ein Hacker. Ich faxe Dir ein Computermagazin. Oder willst Du es vom Internet? Der Cover ist ganz clever. Siehst Du die Liste mit Tips und Tricks? Und mein Foto? Ich bin der grosse Boss hier. Ein Super-Hit. Total cool. Mein Job ist okay, man.

_____

—

_____

—

_____

—

_____

—

_____

—

Although you will hear German like this, it is not considered the best style. And you are most likely to hear it from people under the age of 30.

Wanted: Stolen Words

Thumb through a German dictionary and list other words that are borrowed from English. You will certainly see a lot of words you recognize. Not all of them may have been borrowed from English, though. Some may be common borrowings from Latin, French, or Greek, all of which supplied a huge number of words to both languages. These tend to be cultural words or those of scientific origin.

Some examples of words that both English and German have stolen from other languages include:

das Café (café)

das Cello (cello)

der Brachiosaurus (brachiosaurus)

der Homöopath (homeopath)

die Camouflage (camouflage)

IF YOU'RE SO
INCLINED

To find out more about these words, you can look them up in what is called an *etymological dictionary*. It will tell you all about the origins of a word.

die Passage (passage)

Unfortunately, there is no general rule about the gender of words borrowed from other languages. Note, however, that there are patterns in all words that can help you.

All French-derived words that end in *-et* and *-ment* are neuter in German—with the exception of *der Zement* (cement), *das Ballett* (ballet), and *das Engagement* (engagement). Also, all French words that end in *-age* are feminine in German—with the exception of *die Garage* (garage) and *die Etage* (floor, story).

Be warned, those of you who speak French: Don't try to transfer the gender from French to German. Although many French feminine words stay feminine in German, many French masculine words become neuter in German, such as *das Bonbon* or *das Café*.

Another category of words you will recognize are words borrowed from German into English. These are words that have a certain cultural or historical importance in the German-speaking world. These words include:

Zeitgeist

Angst

Geist

Weltschmerz

Fahrvergnügen

Gastarbeiter

Heimat

Oktoberfest

Realpolitik

Schadenfreude

Vergangenheitsbewältigung

Gemütlichkeit

Waldsterben

Autobahn

Can you think of others?

EXERCISE 4: MAD LIBS

The following little story is just waiting for you to fill in the blanks with cognates. Each blank is marked with a part of speech, such as a noun, adjective, or verb. Find an English cognate of a German word to fill in the blanks. You can use cognates from this chapter or flip through your dictionary. More than one right answer is possible; see the answer key in Appendix D. (Only one version is provided there, however.) Have fun with the story and notice how many cognates there are in German and English, while you are at it.

There once was an (adjective) (adjective) man who was trying to learn German so that he could take a trip to (proper noun) with his (noun). He was very busy at the law (noun), where he was trying to (verb) (noun). His (noun) was a really wonderful (noun) but had no idea how much (noun) and time it takes to raise (noun). His boss insisted that he come in on (plural noun) and late at night to (verb) reports on important cases.

Our blossoming lawyer was a (noun) in patent law. His

clients were (adjective), multinational corporations. In fact, he often (verb) with (plural noun) in Zurich, Munich, and Vienna on the (noun). Their English was so good that it really (verb) him to want to learn more German.

But where could he (verb) the time? A (noun) told him that if he could find excuses, he could find time to (verb). With a (season) vacation trip planned to Germany and Austria, he had great motivation to (verb) at least the basics. Once he got (verb), he was shocked to see how much he already knew. Why had they kept this a secret from him in (noun)?

I promise not to keep any of the secrets of learning German from you. Are you ready to join the secret club of lazy learners? We're too lazy to even have a secret handshake.

Genderbending the German Way: Sex-Crazed Nouns

Yes, nouns in German have grammatical gender. There are masculine, feminine, and neuter nouns. That is one of the big differences between English and German that causes problems for students of the Teutonic tongue. In this chapter, I'll show you the easiest ways to deal with this sexy phenomenon and what it means for nouns you'll use.

NOUN ADVENTURES

I'm not going to bore you with nouns like "chalkboard" or "pupil"; those are words you will rarely need (nor will you enjoy learning them). Instead, let's think of a fun place to be and learn some nouns in that context. Imagine yourself in a snug Alpine cabin. That's where I want you to pretend to be during this lesson. We are going to learn fun nouns that you will enjoy learning and using. When learning a noun, it is important to learn it with its article and its plural form. The article tells you the gender of the word. Dictionaries list the gender and plural form of the word. I've used that convention in this book, too. This is necessary because German plurals are formed irregularly. You'll learn more about that later.

Word World

There are a lot of words to know, but let's start with things you are likely to see around you in a snug alpine cabin or in almost any other room (*Note:* the letters added in parentheses indicate the plural form of the noun; all plurals take "die" as the definite article):

der Tisch(e) = table

der Stift(e) = pen

der Stuhl(ü, e) = chair

der Wein(e) = wine

der Käse(-) = cheese

die Tür(en) = door

die Lampe(n) = lamp

die Uhr(en) = clock

die Postkarte(n) = postcard

das Zimmer(-) = room

das Bild(er) = picture

das Buch(ü, er) = book

das Fenster(-) = window

das Brot(e) = bread

YOU'LL THANK YOURSELF LATER

Note that all nouns in German are capitalized. Always. What could be lazier than recognizing a noun in German? Just look for the capitalized words and you've found them.

How are you going to remember these words? Memorize them in the context of the image of a snug cabin. You may want to write them down or make a drawing of a room and then label it. Enjoy your little alpine adventure. By learning just these few nouns, you have unlocked a key to deciphering long German words, which are really nothing but short ones strung together. The nouns you just learned will provide you with several compounding options, such as *das Bilderbuch* (the picture book) or *das Käsebrot* (cheese bread).

Do you have the preceding list of words down? Okay, now that our lazy little vacation is over, let's get down to some technicalities.

HOW TO LOOK UP A NOUN'S SKIRT

Now that you have learned how to uncover the nouns you already know from the preceding chapter on cognates, let's start on uncovering them in a different way. Notice that I've listed all nouns so far in this book with their article (*der*, *die*, or *das*). Those are the masculine, feminine, and neuter articles, respectively. In general, there is only one way to know a noun's gender: memorization. Some endings and types of words, however, are always a particular gender.

Masculine suffixes identify words that are always masculine:

-ich, as in *der Strich* (line)

-ig, as in *der Käfig* (cage)

-ling, as in *der Dümmling* (dimwit)

QUICK PAINLESS

Always learn the gender and plural of a noun. You will need these grammatical clues every time you use the word, and not having that information will render the word relatively useless.

-or, as in *der Direktor* (director)

-ant/-ent, as in *der Protestant/der Student* Protestant/student)

-ismus, as in *der Kommunismus* (communism)

-ist, as in *der Kapitalist* (capitalist)

-iker, as in *der Physiker* (physicist)

Feminine suffixes identify words that are always feminine:

-ei, as in *die Staffelei* (easel)

-schaft, as in *die Freundschaft* (friendship)

-keit, as in *die Öffentlichkeit* (public)

-tion, as in *die Nation* (nation)

-ung, as in *die Hoffnung* (hope)

-heit, as in *die Freiheit* (freedom)

Neuter suffixes mark nouns that are always neuter:

-lein, as in *das Fräulein* (the young lady)

-chen, as in *das Mädchen* (the girl)

-nis, as in *das Gedächtnis* (memory)

-tel, as in *das Viertel* (quarter)

-um, as in *das Album* (album)

-ier, as in *das Papier* (paper)

Never say "never," and "always" always has an exception. There are a few exceptions to these rules. For example, -tum, as in *das Reichtum* (kingdom), is almost always neuter. It can also be masculine, however, as in *der Reichtum* (wealth).

Add -in for a Sex Change

Adding -in to a noun of occupation makes it feminine:

Masculine Noun	Feminine Noun	English Translation
der Direktor	die Direktorin	the director
der Fahrer	die Fahrerin	the driver
der Kellner	die Kellnerin	the waiter/ the waitress

Feminist Flair

To emphasize the emancipation of women, some feminists write the plural form with a capital *I*; for example, *ÄrztInnen* (women doctors) and *StudentInnen* (female students). These feminine forms of nouns often cannot be translated into English without including the extra word "female" or "women."

Forming the Plural of a Noun

With a few exceptions, forming the plural of a noun in English is simple. You have one computer, and if you are really geeky you have two computers. All you have to do is add an *s* (and a pocket protector). German, on the other hand, has multiple ways of forming a plural; the only sure way to know the right form is to memorize it.

NOUNS AND THEIR JOBS AND HELPERS

Nouns aren't lazy; they work hard. They are used as subjects or objects in sentences. But they can't do their work alone. Among other things, articles accompany them.

You've learned your vocabulary for the day. Now take a break and plan an alpine retreat at home. Fondue is back in style! Or maybe you'd just like to enjoy a cup of Swiss hot chocolate?

The Lazy Way

Those are the helper words, like "the" or "a," that tell whether we are talking about a specific item ("the" is the definite article) or one of many items ("a" or "an" is the indefinite article).

MAKE THE INFLECTION CONNECTION

German is an inflected language. This means that changing the form of the words shows the grammatical function of elements in the sentence. The forms of nouns are called *cases*. The complete table of a noun in all its cases is called a *declension paradigm*. The form of the word "the" you use is the code that tells what function the noun following it has in the sentence.

Here's a mini grammar review. Remember that a sentence must have a subject and a verb. It can also have objects. Don't these terms sound familiar? Let's dissect the patient:

Wir (subject) haben (verb) die (definite article) Lampe (direct object). (Translation: We have the lamp.)

In German, each of these grammatical functions in a sentence is related by the form of the word, known as a case for nouns.

The subject of a sentence is always in the nominative case, which is the "default" you have been learning with the word, as in *die Lampe*.

The direct object of a sentence is always in the accusative case.

Each of these cases requires a different form of "the." That is how we end up with 16 ways to say "the"—three genders, plus one plural, times four cases

equals 16. That sounds daunting, but we'll simplify the matter and work through this one step at a time. With the appropriate form of the simple verb "to have," you can make almost endless sentences about the items in your little alpine chalet.

The following three sentences show the accusative case in action in masculine, feminine, and neuter form:

Wir haben den Tisch. (We have the table.)

Wir haben die Lampe. (We have the lamp.)

Wir haben das Bild. (We have the picture.)

In Case You Were Wondering

Each case plays a different grammatical role. Here is a summary of their jobs:

Cases	Uses
Nominative	Used for subject of a sentence
Genitive	Used to show possession or after prepositions that require genitive objects
Dative	Used for indirect objects or after prepositions that require dative objects
Accusative	Used for direct objects or after prepositions that require accusative objects

QUICK ☐ PAINLESS

The definite article is declined (or grammatically modified) as follows:

	Masculine	Feminine	Neuter	Plural
Nominative				
	der Tisch	die Lampe	das Bild	die Lampen
Genitive				
	des Tisches	der Lampe	des Bilds	der Lampen
Dative				
	dem Tisch	der Lampe	dem Bild	den Lampen
Accusative				
	den Tisch	die Lampe	das Bild	die Lampen

In order to decline and use a noun properly, you must know its gender and its nominative plural. Note that all other cases of a plural noun are based on the nominative form. The dative plural must end in *-(e)n*, even if the nominative does not, however.

The plural is declined as follows:

Nominative	die Tische
Genitive	der Tische
Dative	den Tischen
Accusative	die Tische

Although it may seem crazy that you just had to learn 16 ways to say "the" in German, note that only the masculine article changes between the nominative and accusative cases. The neuter and masculine genitive and dative are also the same. Learn one, and get one free! That's relatively lazy, don't you think?

Practical Practice

The following idyllic folk song will help you practice the notion of the accusative case with a direct object. (*Ich liebe* means "I love.")

> *Ich liebe den Winter, ich liebe den Schnee,*
> *Ich liebe das Eis und den Fluß und den See.*
> *Ich liebe die Blume, ich liebe das Spiel,*
> *Ich liebe die Schule, ich liebe gar viel.*
> *Ich liebe das Bächlein, das Tal und die Höh'n,*
> *Ich liebe die Vögel, sie singen so schön.*

A literal translation yields the following:

> *I love the winter, I love the snow,*
> *I love the ice and the river and the lake.*
> *I love the flower, I love the game,*
> *I love the school, I love so much.*
> *I love the stream, the valley and the peaks,*
> *I love the birds for they sing so beautifully.*

Exercise 1

Complete the following sentences by plugging in the missing definite article. You'll need to consider the proper gender and case for the nouns (for example: *Ich habe den Stuhl*).

Ich habe _____ Tisch.

Ich habe _____ Bild.

Ich habe _____ Stift.

Ich habe _____ Postkarte.

Ich habe _____ Uhr.

Ich habe _____ Lampen.

IF YOU'RE SO INCLINED

Just for fun, run this poem through a translation program. You may be surprised at the results. Some translation programs are available for free on the Web. Check out http://babelfish. altavista.digital.com/ cgi-bin/translate?) What does the output show you?

QUICK ⬛ PAINLESS

Whenever you are learning vocabulary, try to imagine it in context and group items together logically. It'll make them easier to remember.

Exercise 2

And now create your own sentences by translating the following sentences. Use the correct accusative form for the direct object of the sentence.

I have the lamp. _____

I have the heater. _____

I have the table. _____

I have the picture. _____

I have the clock. _____

I have the book. _____

Indefinite Articles

Now let's look at the indefinite article. The indefinite article in English is "a" or "an." It indicates one of many or an "indefinite" choice.

Wir haben einen Tisch. (We have a table.)

Wir haben eine Lampe. (We have a lamp.)

Wir haben ein Bild. (We have a picture.)

Nouns are declined as follows:

	Masculine	**Feminine**	**Neuter**
Nominative	ein Tisch	eine Lampe	ein Bild
Genitive	eines Tisches	einer Lampe	eines Bilds
Dative	einem Tisch	einer Lampe	einem Bild
Accusative	einen Tisch	eine Lampe	ein Bild

There is a pattern here! Again, only the masculine article changes between the nominative and accusative cases. If you are extra lazy, also note that the *-en* ending (which you learned in the chart for definite articles) shows up here again. It is the marker for the masculine accusative.

Exercise 3

Plug in the missing indefinite article into the following sentences (for example: *Ich habe eine Tür.*):

Ich habe _____ Tisch.

Ich habe _____ Bild.

Ich habe _____ Stift

Ich habe _____ Postkarte.

Ich habe _____ Uhr.

Exercise 4

And now create your own sentences by translating the following sentences into German. Remember that direct objects are expressed in the accusative case.

I have a lamp. _____

I have a table. _____

I have a door. _____

I have a clock. _____

I have a book. _____

I have a pen. _____

Take the tension out of the declension. Learn your *der, die, das* table to the tune of a favorite ditty, such as *Happy Birthday*.

The Lazy Way

IF YOU'RE SO
INCLINED

Like those long German words? German compound nouns are simply individual nouns stuck together. You'll see them everywhere once you start looking. The gender of the last word determines the gender of the new compound, like *das Bilderbuch* (picture book).

I Can't Get No Satisfaction

Well, Mick Jagger's English may be more like German than you'd think. *Kein* (not a, not any, or no) is declined like *ein* and can be used in the singular or plural to indicate a lack of something. Hopefully, it won't be satisfaction!

The word *kein* (not a, not any, or no) is declined as follows:

	Masculine	Feminine	Neuter	Plural
Nominative	kein	keine	kein	keine
Genitive	keines	keiner	keines	keiner
Dative	keinem	keiner	keinem	keinen
Accusative	keinen	keine	kein	keine

The word *kein* is used before nouns to indicate that there are none, as follows:

Ich habe kein Zimmer. (I have no room.)

Wir haben keinen Wein. (We have no wine.)

Exercise 5

Translate the following sentences using the correct form of *kein*. For example: They don't have a lamp. (*Sie haben keine Lampe.*)

We don't have a room. _____

You don't have a pen. _____

The room doesn't have a window. _____

I don't have any rooms. _____

Now you know all about nouns, their habits, life cycles, and uses. The good news is that the concepts you learned in this chapter, such as inflection for specific cases, will be useful for other parts of speech as well. This is particularly true for adjectives, which are discussed in the next chapter.

QUICK 🔘 PAINLESS

Kein is used with nouns for negation. For example, *Ich habe kein Essen.* (I don't have any eats.) *Nicht* is used with verbs. For example, *Ich esse nicht.* (I don't eat.)

An On-Ramp to the Adjective Autobahn

What's a language without descriptive words? The lush, round, curvaceous features of a sweet Bavarian automoblle would be indescribable. And its red, white, or metallic gray paint would be flat and colorless. All of these adjectives give life to an image. Unfortunately, many students of German have come to fear the declension of adjectives, which is really just coding them for their grammatical purpose. Well, drop that nonsense right now. First, I'll share the most commonly used adjectives with you. Then, I'll show you how the declensions work with them. You'll be on the adjective autobahn in no time!

ABOUT ADJECTIVES

In German it is categorically imperative for all adjectives to agree with the nouns they modify in gender, number, and case. It is a very "matchy-matchy" language; think loden knickers with a loden jacket, or masculine nominative adjectives with masculine nominative nouns. For example, every time you use a masculine word like der Apfel (apple), you have to use the appropriate adjective to match. To keep things interesting, different endings are used after different types of adjectives and articles. For example, *der grüne Apfel but ein grüner Apfel.* The endings change to indicate a matched set, as you will see in the paradigms presented at the end of this chapter. First, I'll introduce you to adjectives and how to use them the lazy way—without declensions.

AAA Adjectives Vocabulary

First things first! Before you can use adjectives, you have to learn some. The following list includes the most commonly used adjectives in the German language, grouped logically according to categories and with opposites listed next to each other:

gut = good	*schlecht* = bad
groß = big	*klein* = small
schnell = fast	*langsam* = slow
weich = soft	*hart* = hard
teuer = expensive	*billig* = cheap
schön = beautiful	*hässlich* = ugly
alt = old	*neu* = new
heiß = hot	*kalt* = cold
süß = sweet	*sauer* = sour
wichtig = important	*unwichtig* = unimportant
hell = light	*dunkel* = dark
hoch = high	*tief* = deep
laut (loud)	*leise* (soft)

Colors

weiß = white

schwarz = black

rot = red

gelb = yellow

blau = blue

grün = green

orange = orange

lila = purple

If you are going to learn a word, learn an adjective. Nouns you can point at, but descriptive words are harder to pantomime—as anyone who has played charades can tell you. To make learning adjectives easier, try this game. Once you have learned the adjectives in the beginning of this chapter, try to connect the pairs of opposites with a line.

heiß	sauer
neu	langsam
hoch	tief
schwarz	billig
süß	dunkel
teuer	leise
schnell	weiß
laut	alt
hell	kalt

The prefix *un-* is useful in German for making opposites out of many adjectives. For example, the opposite of *freundlich* (friendly) is *unfreundlich*. Your adjective vocabulary can almost double just by adding two letters!

The Lazy Way

THE EASIEST ADJECTIVES

There is, however, one type of adjective that requires no declensions and special endings. When an adjective is used after the verb "to be," or "to become" (so-called auxiliary verbs) to modify the subject, it is called a *predicate adjective*. Reach for a predicate adjective to save yourself some work.

> *Das Haus ist weiß.* (The house is white.)
>
> *Das Auto ist sehr schnell.* (The car is very fast.)
>
> *Ich werde rot!* (I'm turning red!)

Practical Practice

Describe your dream house using the adjectives you have just learned. Keep things simple and use predicate adjectives after the appropriate form of the auxiliary verb *sein* (to be).

For example: Mein Traumhaus ist klein und weiß. Es ist schön. Die Tür ist gelb. Die Fenster sind rot. Mein Haus ist auch alt.

Go ahead. Give it a try!

—

—

—

—

QUICK PAINLESS

If you can't remember the adjective you want, you can use its opposite together with the word *nicht* (not) to get the same meaning. For example: alt = nicht jung, groß = nicht klein.

—

ADVICE ON ADVERBS

Adverbs are used to modify verbs, such as *das Auto fährt schnell* (the car drives fast). As descriptive words, they are often considered alongside adjectives. The good news about German adverbs is that they require no special endings; they are definitely WYSIWYG (what you see is what you get).

Some of the most useful adverbs in German are:

immer = always

jetzt = now

nur = only

schon = already

spät = late

vielleicht = perhaps

wieder = again

Exercise 1

Take a turn familiarizing yourself with adverbs by translating the following sentences into English:

Ich sehe nur Wasser.

_____

Es ist schon Montag.

When you look at many German last names, you can decipher their meanings: *Rotschild* (*rot Schild* = Red Sign) or *Weisshut* (white hat), *Schwarzkopf* (black head), and so on. Open your phonebook and look at how many names now have meaning to you.

_____

Vielleicht ist es das Haus.

_____

Er ist immer schnell.

_____

Jetzt ist es Sommer.

_____

ADJECTIVES WITH ATTITUDE

Now I am going to delve into those times when you'll need to decline your adjectives to agree with the nouns they modify in gender, number, and case. There are three groups of adjective declensions: strong, weak, and mixed. Before you think I am talking about how you'd like your martini (and at this point you may think you need one), let me explain what these terms mean grammatically. I'll work through them one at a time so that you don't get a hangover.

Strong Adjective Declensions

Strong declensions include more data (just like a strong martini) than a weak declension. That means they include the same endings as the table of endings you have already learned for definite articles. (For a review of those, refer to Chapter 7, "Genderbending the German Way—Sex-Crazed Nouns.") The strong declensions are used when no other word shows gender and case or when there is no word other than the adjective preceding the noun. That makes sense because at least one ending in the structure needs to convey the grammatical information of gender, number, and case.

The strong adjective endings are:

	Masculine	Feminine	Neuter	Plural
Nominative	-er	-e	-es	-e
Genitive	-en	-er	-en	-er
Dative	-em	-er	-em	-en
Accusative	-en	-e	-es	-e

Demonstrative Adjectives

Demonstrative adjectives point out which noun is being discussed. For example: "*This* is the cabin." or "*Some* mountains are covered in snow."

dieser, diese, dieses (this)

jeder, jede, jedes (each)

jener, jene, jenes (that)

mancher, manche, manches (some)

solcher, solche, solches (such)

Hurray! Note that the endings for demonstrative adjectives are the same as those you learned already of definite articles.

welcher, welche, welches (which)

They are all declined in the same manner as *dieser*, as follows:

	Masculine	**Feminine**	**Neuter**	**Plural**
Nominative	dieser	diese	dieses	diese
Genitive	dieses	dieser	dieses	dieser
Dative	diesem	dieser	diesem	diesen
Accusative	diesen	diese	dieses	diese

Now you are ready to build demonstrative adjectives into your sentences, such as:

Nominative

Dieser Apfel kommt ist aus meinem Garten.
(This apple is from my garden.)

Genitive

Die Fenster dieser Kirche sind sehr schön.
(The windows of this church are very beautiful.)

Dative

Ich gebe diesem Kind einen Apfel.
(I give this child an apple.)

Accusative

Ich gebe dem Kind diesen Apfel.
(I give the child this apple.)

Exercise 2

Complete the following sentences by adding the endings to the demonstratives provided:

Dies _____ Tage sind schön.

Ich gebe dem Kind dies _____ Apfel.

Ich gebe dies _____ Mann das Brot.

Dies _____ Haus ist groß.

Der Tür dies _____ Autos ist kaputt.

Possessive Adjectives

This useful category will double the return on your investment of learning the adjective endings. Once again they are all the same:

mein, meine, mein (*my*)

dein, deine, dein (*your*, familiar)

sein, seine, sein (*his*)

ihr, ihre, ihr (*her*)

unser, unsere, unser (*our*)

euer, eure, euer (*your*, plural)

ihr, ihre, ihr (*their*)

Ihre, Ihre, Ihr (*your*, formal, singular and plural)

Talk about lazy! All possessive adjectives are declined according to the same pattern:

	Masculine	Feminine	Neuter	Plural
Nominative				
	mein	meine	mein	meine
Genitive				
	meines	meiner	meines	meiner
Dative				

A COMPLETE WASTE OF TIME

The worst thing you can do with possessive adjectives is to not notice the three different meanings of the following look-alike possessive adjectives:

Ihr = your (formal)

ihr = her

ihr = their

Use context (and notice the capitalization of the formal form) to tell them apart.

| meinem | meiner | meinem | meinen |

Accusative

| mein | meine | mein | meinen |

Exercise 3

Now you are ready to take possessive adjectives for a spin. Complete the following sentences by declining the adjective provided:

Sie ist _____ (mein) Mutter. Sie ist die Tochter _____ (mein) Opas. Sie ist auch die Schwester _____ (mein) Tante. In _____ (mein) Familie gibt es keine Kinder.

Weak Adjective Declensions

The weak adjective endings are used when another element in the sentence has an ending that provides the grammatical information about the noun and its function in the sentence. The weak declinations follow these words, which themselves must be declined in the sentence. As in: *Jeder gute Mann ist hier*. Note how the -er ending of *jeder* indicates the nominative masculine nature of "*Mann*."

der, die, das (the)

dieser, diese, dieses (this)

jeder, jede, jedes (each [one])

jener, jene, jenes (that [one])

mancher, manche, manches (a good many)

solcher, solche, solches (such)

welcher, welche, welches (what/which)

Because these particular words impart so much grammatical data on their own, these endings can be much "leaner" or "weaker" in their content and only consist of an -e or -en ending. The following table shows when to use which ending:

	Masculine	Feminine	Neuter	Plural
Nominative	-e	-e	-e	-en
Genitive	-en	-en	-en	-en
Dative	-en	-en	-en	-en
Accusative	-en	-e	-e	-en

Exercise 4: Working "Weak Ends"

Use the weak endings you have just learned to make some strong statements, such as: "*Diese schöne Blume ist eine Rose.* (This beautiful flower is a rose). Now it's your turn. Complete the following sentences by declining the adjective provided:

Der _____ (groß) Mann spielt Basketball.

Dieses _____ (gut) Buch ist auch billig.

Manche _____ (schnell) Autos sind sehr teuer.

Ich habe das _____ (klein) Mädchen.

Wir sind die _____ (best) Studenten.

Mixed Adjective Declensions

The end is in sight! Or should I say ending? The final

category of endings are called the *mixed adjective declensions*. They are called mixed because they combine features from both of the previous declinations. They're a mixed bag, so to speak. The mixed adjective declensions are used after the following words:

ein, eine, ein (a)

kein, keine, kein (no)

mein, meine, mein (my)

dein, deine, dein (your)

sein, seine, sein (his and other possessive adjectives)

You will see that with three exceptions the mixed endings are the same as the weak endings. And, in those three cases, the extra little *-r* or *-s* is needed to show whether the noun is masculine or neuter.

The mixed endings endings are:

	Masculine	Feminine	Neuter	Plural
Nominative	-er	-e	-es	-en
Genitive	-en	-en	-en	-en
Dative	-en	-en	-en	-en
Accusative	-en	-e	-es	-en

Exercise 5: Mix It Up!

Ready to be a mix master? Practice using the mixed adjective endings in the following sentences. For example: *Kein anderer Freund ist so gut.* (No other friend is so good). Now it's your turn. Complete these sentences by declining the adjective provided:

Ich habe ein _____ (alt) Kleid.

Ein _____ (jung) Mann ist hier.

Meine _____ (rot) Rosen sind sehr schön.

Ich habe keine _____ (klein) Rose.

Deine _____ (hell) Jacke ist sehr chic.

Good, Better, Best

Sometimes it is important to be able to compare things. Comparative and superlative adjectives are what you use to fit the bill. The good news is that most of these are formed in a regular manner—like English—by adding -er and -est.

The German comparative is formed as follows:

alt, älter, am ältesten = old, older, oldest

jung, jünger, am jüngsten = young, younger, youngest

The bad news is that, like in English, some of the most commonly used comparative and superlative adjectives are irregular:

groß, größer, am größten = big, bigger, biggest

gut, besser, am besten = good, better, best

hoch, höher, am höchsten = high, higher, highest

nah, näher, am nächsten = near, nearer, nearest

viel, mehr, am meisten = many, more, most

Notice how these comparatives and superlatives are used:

Close cousins offer shortcuts once again! Notice that both English and German form the comparative and superlative by adding -er and -est to the adjective stem. The only tricks to remember are to add an umlaut to the stem in the comparative and superlative forms and "am" before the superlative.

Er ist größer als ich. (He is bigger than I.)

Er ist am größten. (He is biggest.)

Er ist der größte Mann. (He is the biggest man.)

As you can see, when you use a superlative as an adjective, you drop the *am* and decline the superlative stem like any other adjective. Only when it is used as a predicate adjective do you need to use the *am größten* form.

ACTIVE ACTIVITY: CAT IN A HAT

You're ready for a parlor game. Get together with some of your German-speaking friends and try this: Have everyone write the names of well-known Germans on scraps of paper, and place them into a hat. Divide into teams. (The size of the teams can vary with the size of your party.) Have one person from a team draw a name out of the hat, and then describe the famous person using only German words. The first team to guess it gets a point. The team with the most points wins.

Example: Helmut Kohl

Clues: *dick, ehemaliger Bundeskanzler*

Other Germans: Albrecht Dürer, Marlene Dietrich, Martin Luther, Nena, Boris Becker

Get out your fedora and have some fun!

Chapter nine

Do It in German: Having Your Way with Verbs

Don't get tense! I'm going to introduce you to German verbs gently. I'll start with the most common verbs. Then, I'll talk about the differences between the present tense and the past tense. Finally, I'll get back to the future with the future tense.

VERBS: ACTION VERBIAGE

Verbs are words of action or condition. You need them to express things you are, want, or have. Considering there is a nearly endless list of verbs, I will focus on three of the most basic and useful first. Then I'll explore a pattern that will let you crack any verb and bend it to your will.

To Be or Not to Be: The Most Common Verb of All

There's no way to get around it: The most prevalent verb in any language is the verb "to be." German is no exception.

With verbs, if it looks too easy it likely is. Many short verbs are big pitfalls; "come," "put," and "go" are rarely translated literally.

Sein (to be) is the infinitive, or the non-conjugated verb. A *conjugation* is a form of the verb that indicates person and number and tense and mood. Let's define some terms: *First person* means the subject is included in the action (I or we). *Second person* means the subject is addressing the action (You or you all). *Third person* means you are talking about someone who is not part of the conversation (he, she, it, or they). *Number* just means singular or plural. *Tense* means the time of the action. Let's focus on the present tense first. *Mood* means the manner of an action. This book explores only the indicative mood, which is used to express things that are fact, as in "It is a beautiful day" or "I love German." The indicative mood is the most common mood. You can learn the others when you are ready.

Look at how verbs work in English, and then I'll focus on German verbs:

Infinitive: To be

	Singular	Plural
First person	I am	We are
Second person	You are	You all are
Third person	He, she, or it is	They are

Never assume a small, simple phrase is an easy one to translate literally. It is usually short verbs like "put," "get," "make," "do," or "take" that do not translate literally. That is because they tend to be elements of idioms—phrases that are standard in a language and do not translate with one-to-one correspondence.

There are three conjugated forms of the verb "to be": am, is, and are. Notice that they are irregular. That is, they do not follow a pattern (as opposed to a verb like "I sing," "you sing," "he sings," and so on). Therefore, it should not surprise you that the verb "to be" is irregular in German.

Sein (to be)

	Singular	Plural
First person	ich bin	wir sind
Second person (informal)	du bist	ihr seid
Second person (formal)	Sie sind	
Third person	er, sie, es ist	sie sind

The first difference you will notice between German and English in this table are the two forms of "you." *Du* is the informal form for use with friends, family, and children, while *Sie* is the formal form for use with strangers or acquaintances. It is safest to use the *Sie* form until you are asked to use the *du* form. In fact, using the *du* form with someone you don't know well may be considered rude or too informal. Play it safe and stick with *Sie*.

Also, since you're dealing with an irregular verb, there is no other way around it but to learn the various forms. Note, however, that the form for "we," "you" (formal), and "they" is the same. This will always be the case. It's a lazy shortcut; learn one form and you have three covered!

IF YOU'RE SO
INCLINED

The other moods in German are the imperative and subjunctive moods. The *imperative mood* is for giving orders, such as *Seien Sie ruhig!* (Be quiet!) The *subjunctive mood* expresses a manner of condition that indicates politeness, such as *Könnten Sie bitte ruhig sein* (Could you be quiet, please). These are more advanced topics; to learn more, refer to your dictionary's verb tables.

Modal Verbs: Wanting and Being Able

The first verb most children learn is "to want." Just take any two-year-old to a toy store to prove me right! "I want this," "I want that." Adults, of course, learn to be more polite (we hope) and use nicer words. A German child's first verb is likely to be *wollen* (to want), but an adult's is likely to be a form of the verb mögen, such as ich möchte (I'd like to have). *Note:* This is a common irregular verb, and the only trick is to memorize it. The verbs are modal or auxiliary verbs—and they can be used with other verbs, or an object. As in: I like to have ice cream, or I'd like an ice cream. *Mögen* is also likely to be one of the most common words you use or hear when saddling up to an espresso bar in Vienna or touring an auto showroom in Munich. *Was möchten Sie denn gerne?* (What would you like to have?) Here's the scoop on how to decline your wants when *Sie etwas gerne möchten*:

Mögen (like to have)

	Singular	Plural
First person	ich möchte	wir möchten
Second person (informal)	du möchtest	ihr möchtet
Second person (formal)	Sie möchten	
Third person	er, sie, es möchte	sie möchten

Take a break and teach yourself to yodel. Yodeling has its roots in the Alps as a form of communication across distant valleys. Start practicing the break in your voice by singing "yo" and then jumping up an octave and singing "de." The break you hear is a baby yodel. Nurture it to grow into a real yodel with practice. If you need first-hand demonstration, most vocal instructors can show you how it's done. It's a great party trick, and it can't help but make your German seem better. *Ich yodele!*

The Lazy Way

If you're more insistent on wanting something or just trying to be plain rude, you can also holler conjugated forms of the verb *wollen*. (Remember the two-year-old in you!)

Wollen (want)

	Singular	**Plural**
First person	ich will	wir wollen
Second person (Informal)	du willst	ihr wollt
Second person (formal)	Sie wollen	
Third person	er, sie, es will	sie wollen

Exercise 1

Now let's practice using the verb in context. Fill in the blanks in this story about a shopping trip. Use only the conjugated forms of möchten from above.

Emilie _____ eine Lampe. Die zwei Kinder _____ Äpfel. Mein Vater und ich _____ Apfelkuchen und Kaffee. Was _____ du?

While you're at it, you might as well also learn to conjugate the useful modal verbs *können* (to be able) and *dürfen* (to be permitted). These verbs will round out today's lesson in etiquette and politeness.

Können (to be able to/to can)

	Singular	Plural
First person	ich kann	wir können
Second person (informal)	du kannst	ihr könnt
Second person (formal)	Sie können	
Third person	er, sie, es kann	sie können

Dürfen (to be allowed to)

	Singular	Plural
First person	ich darf	wir dürfen
Second person (informal)	du darfst	ihr dürft
Second person (formal)	Sie dürfen	
Third person	er, sie, es darf	sie dürfen

All the preceding verbs have had some irregularities. Now that you have mastered them, let's get down to business and learn a whole list of regular verbs. Let's start out with one of the most common verbs: to make.

Americans tend to "do" things, whereas Germans tend to "make" them. "What are you up to?" is often translated as *Was machst du?* And it is a good thing that

You may! Now that you can say it, give yourself permission to take a break from your German studies! *Sie dürfen eine Pause machen!*

"to make" is a regular verb. What does that mean? Regular verbs follow a strict pattern. The infinitive is the basis for the conjugation, and the rest follows suit. Here's the scoop on *machen* (to make):

Machen (to make)

	Singular	Plural
First person	ich mache	wir machen
Second person (informal)	du machst	ihr macht
Second person (formal)	Sie machen	
Third person	er, sie, es macht	sie machen

The preceding paradigm of all the forms of *machen* uses the regular endings you will see on all other regular verbs. All you need to do is add the endings to the stem of the verb, which you find by dropping the *-en* from the infinitive.

	Singular	Plural
First person	*-e*	*-en*
Second person (informal)	*-st*	*-t*
Second person (formal)	*-en*	
Third person	*-t**	*-en*

*(or *-et* for stems that end in *d* or *t*)

Here's a list of verbs you can use with this regular pattern. These are called *regular verbs*, and conjugating

them is as straightforward as a Swiss train schedule—no exceptions.

> *bringen* = to bring
>
> *finden* = to find
>
> *holen* = to get, fetch
>
> *kaufen* = to buy
>
> *kommen* = to come
>
> *lieben* = to love
>
> *nennen* = to name
>
> *sagen* = to say

Combining Modals

Now that you know a long list of verbs and your modals, you can create a number of sentences by combining the two. Just take the conjugated form of the modal and link it with the infinitive form of the verb.

> *Ich darf es essen.* (I may [am allowed to] eat it.)

Note that the infinitive is always at the end of the sentence, even if the modal verb and subject are inverted—as in a question: *Kannst du kommen?* (Can you come?)

Exercise 2

Translate the following sentences into German:

> I can sleep.

_____

We can go.

_____

Can we buy it?

_____

May we come?

_____

She wants to bring it.

_____

THE PAST TENSE

Naturally, you don't want only to talk about things happening now. You also want to be able to put things in the past tense, as in *Ich war in Frankfurt* (I was in Frankfurt). Sounds a lot like English, doesn't it?

The verb *sein* (to be) is declined as follows in the past tense:

	Singular	Plural
First person	ich war	wir waren
Second person (informal)	du warst	ihr wart
Second person (formal)	Sie waren	
Third person	er, sie, es war	sie waren

Exercise 3

Fill in the verbs in the following story:

1998 _____ ich in Deutschland. München und
Berlin _____ sehr schön. Es _____ Sommer.
Die Tage _____ sehr lange. Wo _____ du
im Sommer 1998? _____ es auch schön?

Now let's look at the past tense of another common verb: *haben* (to have). Here you see the endings you learned for the present tense, but they are preceded by a -*t*-. What could be easier?

The past tense of the verb *haben* is declined as follows:

	Singular	Plural
First person	ich hatte	wir hatten
Second person (informal)	du hattest	ihr hattet
Second person (formal)	Sie hatten	
Third person	er, sie, es hatte	sie hatten

Exercise 4

Use the past tense of the verb *haben* to complete the following sentences:

Ich _____ ein Haus in Berlin.

Wir _____ auch einen Garten.

Er _____ einen Apfelbaum.

BACK TO THE FUTURE

You'll also want to know how to talk about the future, and you can do so by using the future tense. It's easy. Just combine the conjugated form of the verb *werden* with the infinitive of the verb: *Wir werden essen.* (We will eat.) As with modal verbs, the infinitive comes at the end of the sentence. Take a minute to learn the forms of *werden*, and you will be on your way to the future.

	Singular	Plural
First person	ich werde	wir werden
Second person (informal)	du wirst	ihr werdet
Second person (formal)	Sie werden	
Third person	er, sie, es wird	sie werden

Exercise 5

Translate the following sentences into English.

Ich werde es lieben.

_____

Wir werden Berlin sehen.

_____

Du wirst ein guter Freund sein.

_____

Werden Karin und Peter kommen?

_____

Das Baby wird gut sein.

_____

ten

Wordworks: Making Sentences

Grammar: Just mentioning the term calls up images of boring seventh-grade English class and diagramming sentences. Forget that. Once you see that grammar is really a coded structure designed to make communication efficient, you'll be able to turn it into a magic decoder ring. Soon it will be a favorite tool in your growing "lazy way" war chest.

KNOWING YOUR ENGLISH GRAMMAR COLD WILL MAKE YOUR GERMAN HOT

Let's face it: Humans are lazy. (And as you know, this is just another way to say they are efficient!) Throughout the ages we have found it necessary to eliminate superfluous grammatical information. Language needs to get to the point fast. That's where grammar comes in. As a human construct designed to make communication work, our language has come up with quite a few tricks over the years. After all, the ability to speak played a key role in allowing humans to beat out the apes! Commands need to be clear and express meaning unambiguously. Grammar needs to answer the "who is doing what to whom?" question.

Over time, grammar has been simplified and reduced to the essentials without losing any meaning. Once you learn to read this grammatical code, you'll be on your way.

Terminology Talks

A big part of understanding how grammar works is knowing the grammarian's lingo—concepts you'll recognize from English class, such as subjects, verbs, and objects. This terminology is a real shortcut to unlocking the power of language. If there are any terms in the following discussions that you would like to review, just take a quick peek at Appendix C.

Making the Inflection Connection

To understand how German works, you need to realize that the language is held together with a special system of linguistic connectors called *inflection*. German is a highly inflected language, which means that it uses different forms (known as *conjugations* or *declensions*) of words to convey the function of a word in a sentence. This concept is unfamiliar to most English speakers. Modern English uses word order and has only a few instances of inflection. (For example: adding an *s* to the third person singular of a verb, as in I see/he sees.)

This was not always the case, however. In Shakespeare's day, English was much more inflected and similar to German. Look at this example:

A COMPLETE WASTE OF TIME

The three worst things you can do when you are learning German are:

1. Not know your English grammar.

2. Think you can speak German without learning its grammar.

3. Be afraid of grammar. It's just simple definitions and codes that form the traffic rules for a language.

"Thou hast most traitorously corrupted the youth of the realm in erecting a grammar school."

—William Shakespeare in *King Henry VI*, part 2, act 4, scene 7.)

Bill's distaste for school aside, note that "thou" is an antiquated second person singular form of address that sounds very much like the German *du*. (In fact, changing the English *th* to *d* will often give you a German cognate). Don't be surprised, therefore, that the verb conjugation *hast* is the very same as in Shakespearean English and modern German! What about "thou?" English speakers simply got lazy and dropped the initial time-consuming dental fricative *th*, turning the pronoun into the familiar word "you."

GRAMMAR AWARENESS TRAINING

Most people are not always conscious of the grammar rules they use to produce language. How many people can tell you when to use "who" versus "whom?" Knowing some elements of grammar and how they work will make speaking German a matter of plugging in element variables; all you need to do is follow a few rules for word order—or make sure the horse stays in front of the cart.

You may never have noticed before, but there really are a limited number of elements that make up an infinite number of sentences. Now that's what I call lazy!

IF YOU'RE SO INCLINED

You can look into the history of the English language to see its similarities with German. Many similarities have been lost over time, but remnants still remain in familiar Shakespearean language. *Hath* and *hat* really sound alike, don't they? That's because they're related.

Those elements are:

- **Subject:** Generally, the subject of a sentence is the noun or pronoun that performs the action. For example: *Wir* sind Amerikaner. *Hans und Franz* lernen Deutsch. *They* are a bit dense and don't understand grammar too well.

- **Verb:** In broad terms the verb expresses the "action" of a sentence. It can also state a condition, as in "to be," or "to seem." For example: Deutsch *ist* einfach. They *take* their studies seriously. They *become* incorrigible when they don't understand.

- **Object:** An object is the noun or pronoun acted upon by a verb or preposition. There are three types of objects: direct, indirect, and prepositional.

  A *direct object* is a noun or pronoun that directly receives the action of a verb. It answers the questions "what?" or "whom?" asked after the verb. For example: Franz liest *ein Buch*. Hans learns *German* rather slowly. Did you ask *him* why?

  An *indirect object* is a noun or pronoun that indirectly receives the action of a verb: It answers the questions "to whom?," "for whom?," "to what?," or "for what?" asked after the verb. For example: Franz schrieb *der Mutter* einen Brief. He gave *me* his reasons for learning.

  A *prepositional object* is the noun or pronoun that follows a preposition. It answers the question "what?" or "whom?" asked after the preposition. For example: He was never the best student in *his class*. Er lernt fär *die Arbeit*.

- **Complement:** A complement is a noun, pronoun, or adjective that adds meaning to another clause element. A subject complement usually follows the subject and a linking verb such as "to be," "to appear," or "to seem." For example: I am *glad*. Sein Deutsch wird *besser*.

- **Adverbial:** An adverbial expresses a wide range of meanings, including spatial relationship, time, process, respect, contingency, modality, or degree. It answers the questions how, when, why, where, or how much after the verb. For example: I taught him *a little bit*. Er arbeitet *weil er muß*. He lifts weights *in Frankfurt*.

Exercise 1

Diagram the following sentences by underlining the subject, double underlining the verb, and labeling the complements, direct, indirect, and prepositional objects:

We took a trip to Europe last summer.

Our plane landed in Frankfurt. The trip was much too short. I loved Germany. I bought a cuckoo clock for my office. I mailed my friends postcards. I want to go back! Have you been to Germany?

Sentencing Your Elements

These basic elements of grammar form every conceivable sentence in a language. That means there are really only a few basic types of clauses possible. Every other sentence in the language is just a variation on these themes. Efficient or lazy? You decide!

Sentence Element Patterns

Element Pattern	Example
Subject + Verb	*Ich bin.* (I am.)
Subject + Verb + Object	*Ich habe einen Hund.* (I have a dog.)
Subject + Verb + Complement	*Ich bin faul.* (I am lazy.)
Subject + Verb + Object + Object	*Ich gebe dem Hund einen Ball.* (I give the dog a ball.)
Subject + Verb + Object + Adverbial	*Ich habe den Ball in meinem Rucksack.* (I have the ball in my rucksack.)

Orderly Word Order

The elements in the preceding table are used with varying order to ask a question. Just flip around the subject and verb, as follows:

Verb + Subject + Object	*Habe ich den Ball?* (Do I have the ball?)

Asking questions in German is very easy for English speakers because it follows the same pattern.

Exercise 2

Flip the following statements into questions. (For example: Das ist mein Zimmer. Ist das mein Zimmer?)

Das ist mein Auto. _____

Du bist Berliner. _____

QUICK ❍n❍ PAINLESS

The lazy learner can flip any statement into a question by simply switching the position of the subject and the verb.

Sie sind Herr Frank. _____

Das ist meine Telefonnummer. _____

COMPARE AND SAVE

You can save time learning German by comparing it to English and noting the key similarities and differences. You have just seen some of the similarities in how the basic elements of a clause are used; now it's time to look at some of the differences.

English is not a particularly inflected language, which means we don't add a lot of endings to words or change them to alter their case (or grammatical function) in a sentence. There are a few examples of this, however, and speakers of English are most conscious of the case when using pronouns ("He likes me." "I like him.") Here, word order and the form of the pronoun determine the meaning. It is obviously incorrect to say: "Me likes he" or "Him likes I," because the forms "he" and "I" cannot be used as objects of a verb.

There, you just learned to recognize case! And once you understand case in English, you can easily assimilate the German system.

Don't expect the German word order to be the same as it is in English. In fact, think of German as taking this case system to an extreme, which is where the famous expressiveness of German comes in. You see, the more highly inflected a language, the more you can vary word order without losing meaning. And because our brains are programmed to accept language as either being right or wrong, there really is only one correct way to

A COMPLETE WASTE OF TIME

The three worst things to assume in German grammar are:

1. That the word order is the same as in English.

2. That you don't need to learn the correct forms in German.

3. That it isn't logical. It is! Grammar is an elegant system for communicating the functions of the elements in a sentence.

Don't expect natural spoken conversation you overhear in German to be grammatically perfect. Dialects, slang, and shortcuts are common. Even those industrious Germans can be lazy! In fact, some dialects totally omit the dative case. Most educated speakers agree, however, that this is being just a bit too lazy.

inflect words. Otherwise, ambiguities in meaning could occur. And that would be grossly inefficient!

The following is an example of how German and English are different. To change emphasis in German, you can swap around the order of the elements, because the first element in the sentence is considered the most important.

Object + Verb + Subject   *Den Ball habe ich.*
(Literally: The ball
have I!)

Another key difference between German and English word order is that, in German, if anything comes before the subject, the verb and subject must be inverted. It's a key rule, and universally applicable. For example:

Complement +   *Heute bin ich bereit.*
Verb + Subject   (Today, I am ready.)

These are the fundamental rules of word order upon which all sentences in the German language are based. Learn them, and an infinite number of sentences are yours for the taking!

A CASE FOR EVERYTHING AND EVERYTHING IN ITS CASE

You've seen how the elements of a sentence are determined by word order in English, which tells you "who" is doing "what" "to whom." For example:

I give the boy the dog.

In this sentence, *the boy* is the indirect object, or the recipient of the action of the verb. Remember: The indirect object answers "to whom," "for whom," "for what," and "to what."

The dog is the direct object, or the thing being acted upon directly. It answers the question "what" or "whom."

In English, the grammatical function of a word is determined by the position of the word in the sentence. Switch the sentence element order around in the preceding example, and you get: "I give the dog the boy," which is indeed very different from the initial sample sentence.

In German, the same concepts of direct and indirect objects are expressed by using case rather than word order. *Case* is just a fancy word for the function of a word in a sentence. There are two cases in German that you need to look at more closely to understand direct and indirect objects: the *accusative case* and the *dative case*. Remember how tidy Germans are. There is a case for everything and everything must be kept in its case. All direct objects are expressed in the accusative case, whereas all indirect objects are expressed in the dative case. For example:

> *Ich gebe dem Hund den Ball.*
> (I give the dog the ball.)

In this sentence, *dem Hund* is the indirect object, and *den Ball* is the direct object.

Let's look at a declension chart of these words:

Case	Noun
Nominative (subject)	*der Hund* (the dog)/ *der Ball* (the ball)
Dative (indirect object)	*dem Hund/dem Ball*
Accusative (direct object)	*den Hund/den Ball*

DOG GONE DATIVE

The following rhyme will make quick work of cinching the dative and accusative cases:

> The German dative and accusative cases
> Will help your dog get places.
> He's dative if you give him the ball,
> But accusative, if you take him out to call.

In the following sentence, *the dog* is the *indirect object* of the action and, therefore, in the *dative case*:

Ich gebe dem Hund the ball.

In the following sentence, *the dog* is the *direct object* of the action and, therefore, in the *accusative case*:

Ich gehe mit dem Hund auf die Straße.

PERIODICAL POWER

Take a walk to the nearest newsstand and buy a German-language magazine or newspaper. You can start with the easy parts by reading the comics, horoscopes, movie reviews, recipes, or sports scores. Later, you can graduate to the real news. Here are some of the titles you may find: *Die Frankfurter Allgemeine, Die Bild Zeitung, Die Zeit, Die Süddeutsche Zeitung, Der Spiegel, Fokus,* and *Brigitte*. Look at the covers and pick the one that most interests you. You can also access many of these publications on the Internet. See the list of resources at the end of this book for the URLs.

Now that you know how grammar works, you are ready to read some real German. Find the time to get a German periodical and see how much you understand. Your progress in German has been exponential, and you will be amazed at how much you now know. Of course, there is much left to familiarize yourself with; but that will come with time. Learn the basics of grammar well; they are the foundation on which the rest of your language skills will be built.

Gute Mannieren: Poise and Politeness for All Occasions

Germans have a reputation for being somewhat brusque and barging their way to the front of the line (or European history). It's true that it can be each man for himself. You may be surprised to learn, however, that Germans place a great deal of importance on good manners. Minding your manners is easy once you know the rules of the road and some basic vocabulary. Even if you weren't lucky enough to be born with continental charm, soon you'll be able to impress even the most demanding Count or Countess with your knowledge of etiquette and Germanic culture. This chapter will look at the three Cs—conversation, customs, and correspondence—and equip you to tackle them with grace and *gute Mannieren*. You'll be the Prost of the party in no time.

The roots of the German word *höflich* (polite) go back to the word *der Hof* (court, as in the court of Ludwig II), which shows parallel development to the English "courteous."

SMALL TALK IS A BIG DEAL

Pleasantries are an important part of cultural interaction. Luckily, it's very easy to have a mini-conversation. The most commonly exchanged greeting in German is *Guten Tag* (good day). You can say it when you enter a shop, address a customs officer, or make a phone call. If it is before noon, you can also say *Guten Morgen* (good morning). If it's in the evening, you can be ready to say *Guten Abend* (good evening). When someone says one of these to you, be sure to respond in kind. What could be easier? If you are feeling daring, initiate a *Guten Tag* exchange yourself. You'll get one back to be sure. In small towns even people passing on the street exchange a *Guten Tag*. Try it out; you'll fit right in!

If a conversation is initiated, you can double your repertoire by being a good listener and copycat. You will be able to turn the sentences your partner gives you around and recycle the words. In many cases, this conversation management strategy enables you to bridge the gap between your passive and active knowledge. You just have to remember a word long enough to use it in your reply. You'll also make it easier on yourself if you let the other person do most of the talking. What could be more polite?

THE LITTLE THINGS

The little things often make all the difference. This section looks at some of the cultural nuances you'll want to understand.

Be on Time

Punctuality is a virtue. Being on time is of great importance to Germanic people. Trains and buses run like Swiss watches; being late means missing them. Meetings start on time, and you should arrive on time when you are invited to a social event.

Shake It

When you are introduced and names are exchanged, be sure to shake hands. This formal method of greeting is considered the appropriate way to say hello. If you are visiting parts of Austria, ladies, don't be surprised if a gentleman actually kisses your hand. And men, if you want to "go native," don't smack the back of your hostess's hand, but rather the air right above it.

At the Table

Generally, meals in Germany are proceeded by a toast. The host will raise his glass and say *Prost*. Raise your glass and look the host in the eye as you sample the local beverage of choice. Now wish your tablemates a *Guten appetit* (good appetite), and let the games begin!

One of the charming parts of meals in Germany is the great array of cold cuts, cheeses, and marmalades that adorn the table. Before you reach right in and practice your "boarding school reach," ask someone to pass a dish to you. Just point and say *Das da, bitte* (That there, please). Also, be sure to use the fork provided with the platter, not your own, to spear those delicate herring balls. Watch the host for cues how to navigate the

YOU'LL THANK YOURSELF LATER

Unless you are willing to listen to a long list of ailments and health details, don't ask the American standard question of "How are you?" (*Wie geht es Ihnen?*). This has really become a stock phrase in English that almost doesn't require an answer. In German, however, the question is taken rather literally. Do yourself a favor and just don't go there.

utensil pitfalls. For example, Germans don't eat their open-faced sandwiches with their hands; they dissect them with a fork and knife.

You'll also note that Germans hold the fork in their left hand and eat with the tines down, which may look a bit strange at first but is actually very practical and elegant if done correctly.

HAPPY HOLIDAYS

Germans know how to celebrate. (Just ask anyone who has survived Munich's celebrated Oktoberfest, which is attended by thousands each year!) Calendar highlights are the traditional holidays of Christmas, Easter, and New Year's. Predominately Catholic regions (the South) have additional extensive church holidays, from Ascension to Whitsun. Mind you that all of these *Feiertage* (holidays) mean no school, no work, and no shopping. (And that's on top of the standard German's six weeks of paid vacation annually.) It's no wonder the Germans have time to celebrate well.

The most stunning holiday in Germany is Christmas. Perhaps it is the snow-peaked mountains or the beautiful concerts that will delight your heart. Regardless, Christmas is a holiday not to be missed! In the weeks before Christmas, you can expect city squares to be brimming with holiday cheer in the form of *Weihnachtsmärkte* (Christmas markets)—the most famous of which is in Nuremberg. Miniature cities of booths with wooden roofs are set up so that artists can

YOU'LL THANK YOURSELF LATER

If you learn only one German word, it should be *danke* (thank you).

sell their Christmas crafts. Even if you are not in the shopping mood, you can't go wrong with a glass of *Glühwein* (mulled wine) or a *Lebkuchen* (a spicy cookie made of candied fruit, nuts, and gingerbread).

On Christmas Eve, Germans celebrate by exchanging gifts in the soft glow of real candles on a *Tannenbaum* (Christmas tree). Singing is a joyous part of the evening, with many favorites such as *O Tannenbaum* and *Stille Nacht*. Many a Yuletide feast includes a roasted goose. The evening is often rounded out with a midnight church service. The next two days are holidays. The world is relatively quiet between Christmas and New Year's Eve (*Sylvester*), which Germans celebrate with a bang—a bang of fireworks, that is.

Birthdays are also taken seriously and celebrated thoughtfully with calls and cards from friends. Some saint name days are also celebrated by their namesakes in Catholic regions.

Holiday Vocabulary

Impress your German contacts by politely wishing them happy celebrations:

Frohe Weihnachten! (Merry Christmas!)

Gutes Neues Jahr! (Happy New Year!)

Frohe Ostern! (Happy Easter!)

Alles Gute zum Geburtstag! (Happy Birthday!)

YOU'LL THANK YOURSELF LATER

When in Germany, don't announce your birthday unless you want to. Traditionally, the one who's celebrating picks up the tab.

GRACEFULLY OVERCOMING THE LANGUAGE BARRIER

Yes, there will be occasions when the language barrier seems insurmountable. The trick is to stay calm and use some strategy to get the job done. Here are some ideas to make the worst-case scenarios bearable.

When you get stuck and want to speak English, don't just launch into it. Ask politely whether your audience speaks English. *Sprechen Sie Englisch?* Then continue slowly and clearly in English. Remember that most Germans understand some English from their school days, but they may not understand you if you use slang or talk fast. Go slow and try to use common words. You'll find that if you use words of German origin, you may be better understood; the cognate effect will help your listener.

You may also want to return the favor by welcoming visitors to speak German on your home turf. Make a sign for your front door or office that says *Wir sprechen Deutsch* or *Willkommen!* See who stops by; you may be surprised.

ON YOUR MARK, GET SET, SPEND

D Mark, that is! The *Deutsch Mark* (DM) is the currency of the Federal Republic of Germany. Austria uses the *schilling* (AUS), which is divided into 100 *groschen*; Switzerland uses the *Swiss franc* (CHF). You'll want to know a few vocabulary words to help you spend your traveler's checks.

You've worked hard. Now it's time to impress a friend or colleague by sending an appropriate card or greeting in German. Pick one from the list in this chapter. Casually mention that you are learning German in your spare time and have found that the language is not as hard as people say.

The Lazy Way

Money Talks

The following phrases will help you get across your financial intentions:

Wieviel kostet das? = How much does that cost?

kosten = to cost

kaufen = to buy

verkaufen = to sell

wechseln = to exchange

das Geld = money

die Münze = coin

das Papiergeld = paper money

der Reisescheck = traveler's check

die Kreditkarte = credit card

der Geldautomat = automatic teller machine

die Bank = bank

der Wechselkurs = exchange rate

das Trinkgeld = tip

das Kleingeld = change

Common Conversation

Here's an example of a common exchange you might have with someone at an information booth:

Tourist	*Wo kann ich Geld wechseln?* (Where can I change money?)
Auskunft (Information)	*Wir haben eine Bank und ein Geldautomat.* (We have a bank and an automatic teller machine.)

A COMPLETE WASTE OF TIME

The three worst things you can do with dialect are:

1. Try to go native. A few words of greeting are fine for local color, but don't pretend you were born there.

2. Use it instead of "high German." It may be easier to slur your endings or add *-le* (Swabian) or *-li* (Swiss German) to a noun to make it an automatic neuter, but don't.

3. Think you'll understand all of it. Some dialects are so different from "high German" that even native speakers don't understand them.

Tourist	*Was ist der Wechselkurs?* (What is the exchange rate?)
Auskunft	*Heute ist der Dollar bei 1.67.* (Today the dollar is at 1.67.)
Tourist	*Danke!* (Thank you!)
Auskunft	*Auf Wiedersehen!* (Goodbye!)

TROUBLE-FREE TEMPLATES

Correspondence in a foreign language can give anyone writer's block. Overcome it the lazy way by using the following templates to confirm a reservation or to thank a friendly host, for example. You can customize the letters and their translations to fit your needs.

We're Buying It!

Sehr geehrte Damen und Herren,

Ich möchte bestätigen, daß ich am 1. Mai 2003 bei Ihnen unseren Wagen/unseren Einkauf abholen werde. Ich würde gerne auch eine kleine Führung in Ihrer Stadt/in Ihrem Werk haben. Können Sie mir eine bieten? Bitte bestätigen Sie diesen Termin.

Mit freundlichen Grüßen,

Dear Sir or Madam,

I would like to confirm that I will pick up our car/our purchase on May 1, 2003. I would also like to have a brief tour in your city/your factory. Could you provide one? Please confirm this date.

With kind regards,

In German restaurants, the tip is included in the price of the meal. Just round up to the nearest even amount when getting your change, and you will adequately thank your server.

We're Grateful

San Francisco, den 1. Dezember 2000

Sehr Geehrte Frau Schmidt,

Ich möchte mich bei Ihnen für das Geschenk/die Unterkunft/das Essen/den schönen Tag bedanken. Unseren Aufenthalt bei Ihnen in Köln/München/Berlin werden wir nie vergessen. Anbei finden Sie ein paar Fotos. Melden Sie sich wenn Sie mal in Amerika sind. Wir würden uns gerne revangieren. Unsere Addresse ist Familie Jones, 555 Mission Street, San Francisco, CA 55555, USA. Tel. (+1) 555-555-5555, Email: hock@555.com.

Ihre,

Dear Ms. Schmidt,

I would like to thank you for the present/accommodations/food/lovely day. We will never forget our stay with you in Cologne/Munich/Berlin. Enclosed please find a few photographs. Please contact us if you come to the United States. We'd like to return the favor. Our address is: Jones Family...

Yours,

We're Coming

Sehr geehrte Damen und Herren,

Meine Frau und ich werde am 1. Dezember 2002 in Hamburg sein. Wir hätten gern ein Doppelzimmer/ein Einzelzimmer mit/ohne Bad für

A COMPLETE WASTE OF TIME

When addressing a German never, but never:

1. Use the *du* form unless you are invited to do so. It is always okay with children or animals, however.

2. Call someone by his or her first name Always use *Frau Schmidt* or *Herr Bauer* until asked to do otherwise.

3. Dispense with titles. Even holders of non-medical doctorates are addressed as *Herr* or *Frau Doktor*.

eine Nacht/zwei Nächte. Bitte schicken Sie uns eine Preisliste, eine Brochüre und eine Bestätigung. Wir freuen uns auf unseren Besuch!

Mit freundlichen Grüßen,

Dear Sir or Madam,

My wife and I will be in Hamburg on December 1, 2002. I would like to reserve a double room/single room with/without private bath for one night/two nights. Please send us your rates, a brochure, and a confirmation of our reservation. We look forward to our visit!

With kind regards,

SLING SOME SLANG

Variety is the spice of life. Now that you know how to be a goodie two-shoes in German and mind your manners, it might be fun to learn a few more colloquial terms.

The Good

As you can see from the following German slang terms, being good is considered a "racy" condition:

> *toll* = great (literally, *crazy*)
> For example: *Der BMW 540 ist ein tolles Auto!*
> (The BMW 540 is a great car!)

geil = hot, fantastic (literally, *horny*)

For example: *Es gibt geile Kneipen in Berlin.*

(There are hot bars in Berlin.)

Mega-cool = really cool.

For example: *Deutsche Technomusik ist mega-cool.*

(German techno-music is really cool.)

The Bad

Knowing a few good ways to dress down a bad situation can put you in a stronger negotiating position:

doof = stupid

For example: *Keine doofe Hausarbeit, bitte!*

(No stupid homework, please!)

blöd = stupid

For example: *Bin ich blöd, oder was?* (Am I stupid, or what?)

krass = harsh

For example: *Die Prüfung gestern wahr echt krass.*

(The test yesterday was really harsh.)

sau blöd = really dumb (literally, pig stupid)

For example: *Meine Lehrerin ist sau blöd.*

(My teacher is really dumb.)

Schluß mit lustig = that's enough fun

For example: *Schluß mit lustig; ich trinke nur noch deutsches Bier.* (That's enough fun; now I'm going to drink only German beer.)

QUICK 🔲 PAINLESS

If the thought of changing money and traveler's checks during your trip scares you, just charge it! Most places accept major credit cards. When you can't use plastic, pay with cash from an ATM machine. Check with your bank before going to make sure you can access your funds.

The Automobile

A favorite topic with Germans is their cars. It should come as no surprise that they have pet names for them:

die Kiste = neutral term for a car (literally, box)
For example: *Meine alte Kiste fährt noch.*
(My old car still runs.)

der Schlitten = complimentary term for a car
(literally, sled)
For example: *Er hat einen schnellen Schlitten.*
(He has a fast automobile.)

die Karre = heap
For example: *Bernds alte Karre ist rot.*
(Bernd's old heap is red.)

der fahrbare Untersatz = set of wheels
For example: *Kannst du mir einen fahrbaren Untersatz liehen?* (Can you loan me a set of wheels?)

twelve

Doing Deutschland: From the North Sea to the Blue Danube

You are ready to plan your big trip to German-speaking Europe. What will your itinerary include? This chapter will start with an overview of the regions and then touch on some of the highlights while you learn some of the key vocabulary and grammar structures you'll need to make your travel communications run as smoothly as a Swiss train schedule. Speaking of punctuality, you'll also learn how to tell time. Now you have the excuse you've been looking for to buy a Swiss watch, right?

MAPPING IT OUT

The German-speaking world mainly consists of Germany, Austria, and Switzerland. However, regional identity is of prime importance to most German speakers; someone in Munich is likely to say he is a Bavarian first and a German

second. This strong sense of regionalism is the lingering result of the Germanic tribes that held central Europe more than 1,000 years ago and the resulting political patchwork. (Remember those Saxons and Franks from history class?) These tribes were the ancestors of today's Germans, Austrians, and Swiss, and this heritage expresses itself today in local dialects, customs, and architecture. In fact, Hamburg and Vienna are much more different than, say, Toronto and San Francisco.

Local Color

When you move from region to region, you will notice that even the simplest things change. Hello is hello is hello, right? Well, it is not quite that simple in German. This chart shows the regional greetings and words of thanks that you will encounter in different parts of the German-speaking world:

Region	Hello	Goodbye	Thank You
North	Guten Tag!	Tschüs!	Danke!
Bavaria	Grüß Gott!	Servus!	Danke!
Austria	Grüß Gott!	Servus!	Danke!
Switzerland	Grüezi!	Auf Wiederluagen!	Merci!

The unique characteristics of the various regions of the German-speaking world are what will make your trip so interesting. Americans often find the scale of Europe surprisingly small. Germany is just a bit smaller than Montana; Switzerland is about the size of Connecticut; and Austria is roughly the size of Maine.

Although it is much smaller than the United States, the German-speaking world offers an abundant wealth of cultural heritage. You could spend literally years traveling around and still not see everything. The cultural differences are very apparent from region to region, making for interesting exploration. With that in mind, let's put together a sample lazy itinerary that will introduce you to the tops and pops of German culture.

Touring Germany

Starting the tour in the northern port city of Hamburg, you'll find fish markets along the harbor, the racy "Reeperbahn" red light district for salty sailors, and a busy commercial city with more bridges than Amsterdam and Venice combined. After a history of being raided by Vikings from the north, Hamburg was a founding member of the Hanseatic League. Early to embrace the reformation, Hamburg and most of the population in northern Germany remain Protestant today. Although northerners have the reputation for being cold and stern compared to the jolly, beer-loving Bavarians, you will not find them to be as cold as the North Sea winds that blow through the charming alleys lined with gabled red-brick houses. In fact, northern Germans are known for their dry sense of humor.

Are you ready to explore your German surroundings? Learn some words that will help you with your orientation:

die Autobahn = freeway

das Dorf = village

QUICK PAINLESS

Learn the names and common abbreviations for the three German-speaking countries: Germany: *Deutschland* (D), Austria: *Österreich* (A), and Switzerland: *die Schweiz* (CH). The *CH* stands for Confoederatio Helvetica, after the Celtic Helvetii who came to the region almost 2,000 years ago. The Latin name *Helvetia* is used on Swiss money and stamps.

die Grenze = border

die Hauptstadt = capital (literally, main city)

die Stadt = city

der Stadtplan = city map

die Straße = street

die Reise = trip

Then it is off to Berlin. The reunited capital is a cosmopolitan city with a population of 3.5 million. Always a haven for the avant-garde, art and money mix as Berlin is now bolstered by an influx of corporations making it their German headquarters. Add to the mix the influx of national government and more Turkish families than any city outside of Turkey, and you have a mix that is both volatile and exciting at the same time.

The physical changes in Berlin have been quicker to heal than the psychological ones of a prolonged division. Although you can get a sense of the impact of the *Mauer* (wall) by visiting the Checkpoint Charlie museum, the "no man's land" that was once patrolled by guard dogs is now a booming construction zone.

Berlin's major attractions are the world-class museums that feature art and treasures from around the world. A lazy day treat not to be missed is a sunny afternoon lounging at the lovely lakes surrounding the city. Of course, Berlin is also famous for its nightlife—if you can muster enough energy to keep up with the club hoppers dressed head to toe in obligatory Berlin black.

Munich, the capital of Bavaria, is a favorite stop for beer stein collectors and tourists alike. But seriously, there is much more to *München* than Oktoberfest and the Hofbräuhaus. A tree-shaded Biergarten is the summer quaffing choice of the locals. Theater, opera, and film have a rich tradition here. Munich is home to the BMW factory and museum, just one example of its booming industry. On a clear day you can see the Alps from downtown. Munich is a great starting point for alpine skiing and hiking excursions. Munich's skyline is punctuated with the spires and domes of beautiful catholic churches.

Down the Danube

Austria is next on the itinerary. Salzburg, Innsbruck, and Vienna are wonderful cities to visit. You'll soon come to love the tradition of spending a quiet afternoon with *Kaffee und Kuchen* in a quaint café. Follow that up with an evening concert of Mozart's music or an opera, and you may never want to leave. (I have often wanted to stay on a bit longer, especially after sleeping under a cozy down comforter that seems at least a foot thick.)

Austria's history is very separate from that of Germany. The heyday of the Austro-Hungarian Empire ended with World War I. The Anschluß of Austria to Hitler's Germany in 1938 also resulted in major Western influences over Austria's post-war history. A country of just eight million people, *Österreich* has some of the most beautiful countryside in the world. Not surprisingly, tourism is a major part of the country's economy, with visitors coming for music festivals, winter sports, and summer hiking.

IF YOU'RE SO
INCLINED

If you want to open a brewery in Germany, you'll have to heed the *Reinheitsgebot* (beer purity laws) of 1516. In addition to water, you can use only three ingredients: hops, yeast, and barley.

Up in the Alps

The last stop on the tour is Switzerland. Although it is politically neutral, if arsenals were stocked with chocolate, Switzerland would be deadly! Four official languages are spoken within Switzerland's borders: German, French, Italian, and Romansch. The Swiss speak a very distinct dialect of German called *Schwyzerdütsch* (Swiss German). It is a charming, sing-song language, featuring many words that end in *-li* (the Swiss version of the German diminutive *-lein*). However, most writing and radio and television programs are presented in high German in the German-speaking part of the country. (French, Italian, and Romansch are also official languages in Switzerland.) You'll be able to understand the Swiss if they slow down and speak *Schriftdeutsch* (written German) for you.

For a country with limited natural resources, Switzerland has certainly made a major impression on world commerce by becoming the banking and insurance capital of the world.

Zurich's old town is a good place to start exploring Switzerland. From the swank shops along the *Bahnhofstraße* to the snug cafés in the old town along the Limmat River, you'll find that the Swiss are very proud of their tidy environs. Red geraniums festoon window boxes, and snow-peaked mountains rise behind mountain lakes. If anywhere in the world looks better in real life than it does in the postcards, it's Switzerland.

Now that you have reviewed your geography and are ready to embark on a tour of Switzerland, prepare your taste buds with a bar of delicious Swiss milk chocolate.

The Lazy Way

FROM HERE TO THERE

Getting around will be a big part of your trip. Whether you travel by plane, train, or automobile, you will want to know the verb *fahren*. It means to drive or travel and has many uses, as you will see. The verb *fahren* is a strong verb. That is, the stem changes in the second and third person singular from *a* to *ä*. Otherwise, it is regular in its forms.

Fahren (to drive)	Singular	Plural
First person	ich fahre	wir fahren
Second person	du fährst	ihr fahrt
	Sie fahren	sie fahren
Third person	er, sie, es fährt	sie fahren

What good is traveling if you can't get there from here? The structure *fahren von X nach X* is very useful when you want to explain where you are going. *Nach* can be used before city and country names (except those that take an article; they use *in*). The preposition *in* requires an object in the accusative case when indicating motion toward something. Note that the preposition *von* takes a dative object. City names never have an article, of course, so there's no need to worry about cases. How much easier could it be to get from one place to the next?

You can see these cases in action in the following sentences:

Er fährt von Berlin nach Potsdam. (He's driving from Berlin to Potsdam.)

QUICK PAINLESS

When you need information, look for signs with a big letter *I* in a circle. This is the international symbol for "Information" and will usually lead you to a useful map or information booth.

Wir fahren von München in die Schweiz. (We're driving from Munich to Switzerland.)

Exercise 1

Now it's your turn. Take a theoretical trip and translate the following sentences:

We're traveling from Hamburg to Berlin.

_____

I am going from Switzerland to Austria.

_____

He's traveling from Germany to Switzerland.

_____

She's traveling from Cologne to Frankfurt.

_____

Exercise 2

Place names often have different names in German and English. You will be able to decipher most of them by making an educated guess. Get some practice by matching the following:

Österreich	Zurich
Donau	Cologne
die Schweiz	Danube
Braunschweig	Bavaria
Bayern	Munich
München	Nuremberg
Nürnberg	Austria

YOU'LL THANK YOURSELF LATER

Get ready to use the metric system; it's the European standard. The following are three of the most useful measurements:

1 kilometer = .62 miles

1 liter = .26 gallons

1 meter = 3.28 feet

Köln	Westphalia
Wien	Switzerland
Zürich	Vienna
Westfalen	Cologne
Rhine	Brunswick

TELLING TIME

To quote the old German couple in Casablanca, "What watch?" "Such much?" Keeping time in German requires some new idioms. If you want to know the time, ask:

Wie spät ist es? (What time is it?)

To respond with the time, you can use the system associated with digital clocks and schedules; for example, *sechs Uhr siebenundzwanzig* (six twenty-seven). This way, you can avoid the fancier structures.

The following examples show how time is discussed:

Wie spät ist es? (What time is it? Literally, how late is it?)

Es ist zehn Uhr. (It is ten o'clock. Literally, it is ten watch.)

Wann fährt der Zug? (When does the train go?)

Er fährt um zwölf Uhr dreißig. (It goes at twelve-thirty.)

You'll notice that Europeans keep track of the hours by using the military clock. They abandon the A.M./P.M. system and call 1:00 P.M. 13:00 (*dreizehn Uhr*), 2:00 P.M. 14:00 (*vierzehn Uhr*), and so on.

YOU'LL THANK YOURSELF LATER

The one question most people want to know before going to Munich is how to ask for a beer. Ask for *Ein Maß, bitte!* and you'll get a liter stein of foamy brew. In the rest of Germany, ask for *Ein Bier, bitte!*

Red Baron Arrivals

More travel time is spent at airports than anywhere else, it seems. Get ready to know the territory by learning the vocabulary you'll need for the airport and transfers:

die Abfahrt = departure

die Ankunft = arrival

der Aufzug = elevator

der Ausgang = exit

das Auto = car

der Bus = bus

die Bushaltestelle = bus stop

der Bahnhof = train station

die Ecke = corner

der Flug = flight

der Koffer = suitcase

der Paß = passport

die Straßenbahn = streetcar

das Taxi = taxi

der Taxistand = taxi stand

die Toilette = restroom

der Zoll = customs

der Zug = train

links = left

rechts = right

Take Me to Your Leader

I'll take one of these and one of those hand verbs, please. Once you know the verb *nehmen* (to take), you can use it with nouns to express how you travel, because it is used together with modes of transportation.

Nehmen (to take)	Singular	Plural
First person	ich nehme	wir nehmen
Second person	du nimmst	ihr nimmt
Third person	er, sie, es nimmt	sie nehmen

Ich nehme ein Auto. (I take a car.)

Ich nehme einen Bus. (I take a bus.)

Ich nehme eine Straßenbahn. (I travel by streetcar.)

Ich nehme ein Taxi. (I take a taxi.)

Ich nehme einen Zug. (I take a train.)

Finding and Falling into a Feather Bed

Why don't men ever ask for directions? Probably because they don't want to find out they are wrong! You should not hesitate to ask for directions when looking for your hotel; it can save tons of time and frustration.

Don't be afraid to ask! Remember: The verb comes right after the question word, as in the following examples:

Wo ist das Hotel? (Where is the hotel?)

Wo ist der Bahnhof? (Where is the train station?)

QUICK ⬤ PAINLESS

Cash in on student, teacher, and senior discounts by getting an international ID card before you go to Europe. Check with your school or college for details.

Practical Practice

Read the following dialog aloud while you imagine yourself carrying two heavy suitcases and having jet lag (just kidding):

Tourist	Wo ist das Hotel Regenberger?
Information	Das Hotel ist in der Sonnenbergstraße. Sehen Sie, hier auf dem Stadtplan.
Tourist	Soll ich ein Taxi nehmen?
Information	Ja. Ein Taxistand ist links um die Ecke.
Tourist	Danke.
Information	Bitte. Auf Wiedersehen!

Mission Accomplished, Hotel Secured

Now that you have found your hotel, make sure you get what you want. The following handy words will guarantee you get a feather bed in no time:

der Ausblick = view

das Bad(ezimmer) = bath(room)

die Badewanne = bathtub

der Balkon = balcony

das Bett = bed

die Bettdecke = blanket

der Bügeleisen = iron

das Doppelbett = double bed

die Dusche = shower

das Fernsehen = television

des Handtuch = hand towel

IF YOU'RE SO INCLINED

Use the following template to create a card you can use at check-in for all your hotel stays:

Mein Name ist Smith, John. Ich möchte ein Einzelzimmer/Doppelzimmer mit/ohne Bad/WC/ Dusche für eine Nacht/ zwei/drei/vier Nächte. Ich möchte (kein) Frühstück.

(My Name is Smith, John. I would like a single/double room with/without bath/toilet/shower for one night/two/three/four nights. I want (no) breakfast.)

die Heizung = heater

das Kopfkissen = pillow

der Schlüssel = key

die Seife = soap

das Telefon = telephone

der Wecker = alarm clock

das Zimmer = room

brauchen = to need

packen = to pack

schlafen = to sleep

tragen = to carry

warten = to wait

zahlen = to pay

JUST GOT TO HAVE IT

When you need something, you'll really benefit from the verb *brauchen* (to need). There are some things you've just got to have:

Brauchen (to need)	Singular	Plural
First person	ich brauche	wir brauchen
Second person (informal)	du brauchst	ihr braucht
Second person (formal)		Sie brauchen
Third person	er, sie, es braucht	sie brauchen

YOU'LL THANK YOURSELF LATER

You can reduce stress by staying at accommodations that match your budget. This is where knowing some key terminology comes in handy. Here are your options, from least to most expensive: *Jugendherberge* (youth hostel), *Pension* (boarding house), *Gasthaus* (guest house), *Hotel*, or *Hof* (court; usually a very plush place to crash with a price to match). Bring along any copies of confirmations for hotel or car reservations on your trip. You can present them at the front desk rather than going through all the details again.

Expect the Wurst: Order the Best

German cuisine is often maligned in travel literature, coming in just ahead of the English attempts. This is nonsense. The various regions of Germany offer their own specialties and have been strongly influenced by their more famous culinary neighbors, France and Italy. In this chapter, I tell you the words you'll need to know to find a restaurant in your budget and then order what you like, whether you are a vegetarian or a fan of *Hasenpfeffer*. Along the way, I tell you about the tops and pops of fresh German bread and other regional specialties you'll want to try on your trip. And finally, I'll encourage you to plan and execute a German meal all by yourself. It's good practice, and you have to eat dinner anyway, right?

FROM ZERO TO THREE STARS

Knowing which eateries offer which type of service will quickly help you decide where to go for dinner. You often can tell

the different categories simply by looking at the name of the establishment. Here are some of the most popular types, from least to most expensive:

der Stehimbiß = snack bar

das Café = café

der Lokal = pub

das Gasthaus = guest house

das Restaurant = restaurant

Perhaps you are a traveler who never steps off the Concorde without a copy of *Zagat's* restaurant survey in hand. If you land somewhere in between, however, you may find the city's Ratskeller to be the safest bet. The *Ratskeller* (literally, Council's Cellar) is the restaurant in the basement of a town's city hall. Generally, these places are nice establishments with traditional German fare. Regardless, you'll need to ask directions to find the best place for a romantic dinner for two or just the nearest hot dog stand.

Exercise 1: Foraging for Food

Before you can eat it, you have to find it. Asking the natives for help is a snap with this simple structure:

Entschuldigung, wo ist ein gutes Restaurant? (Excuse me, where is a good restaurant?)

You can substitute the name of the restaurant or a different type of eating establishment as well. Notice how the verb (*ist*) comes directly after the question word (*wo*). The following exercise gives you a chance to practice all the useful adjectives from Chapter 8, "Fast or Slow, Red or White—An Onramp to the Adjective Autobahn."

Ask where the following eateries are located. (For example: *Entschuldigung, wo ist das Gasthaus zum Hirsch?*)

A warm café

_____

An inexpensive pub

_____

The nearest restaurant

_____

The Ratskeller

_____

The Hofbräuhaus

_____

Daily Bread

If you are not up for a full meal but want more of a snack, head to a *Bäckerei*; you will not be disappointed. The phrase "Give us our daily bread" takes on a new meaning when you realize there literally are enough different types of bread in the German-speaking world for you to eat a different one every day of the year. You'll find all of them at a *Bäckerei*, along with delicious simple desserts.

QUICK  PAINLESS

Before starting a meal, wish your companions *Guten Appetit!* It's the German equivalent of *Bon Appetit!* and a common mealtime ritual.

The basket of bread on the table at a restaurant is not included in the price of the meal. Help yourself, but know that the number of rolls you consume will be duly counted and added to your bill.

The most cherished institution of all is perhaps the *Brötchen* (or little bread)—a roll served with most meals and the cornerstone of a German breakfast. There are endless variations on the theme, and all of them are excellent. Note that in Bavaria the same warm puffs of wheat are called *Semmel*.

For really fancy cakes, head to a *Konditorei* (confectioner's shop). Between 3 o'clock and 5 o'clock in the afternoon, you can join elderly ladies in hats and gloves for their cherished *Kaffee und Kuchen*.

At either shop, you'll be in awe of the selection. The glass cases just seem to go on and on. What's a hungry traveler to do? The best strategy (and the one used by locals) is to point and say, *Eins davon, bitte* (One of those, please). If you want two of something, simply say, *Zwei davon, bitte*.

Bread Basics

From dark to light to horse's delight, you can find something for the carbo lover in you. Learn the following standard bread types and show some flour power:

- *Finnenbrot:* A multigrain bread made with sunflower seeds

- *Vollkornbrot:* A whole wheat bread, usually made with six grains

- *Roggenbrot:* A rye bread

- *Schwarzbrot:* A black, deadly-when-thrown bread

- *Weißbrot:* A white bread

Going to the Grocery Store

If you are after raw ingredients or want to stock your Rucksack for a hike, go to a grocery store. There are some key differences between European markets and supermarkets in the United States, however.

The most important rule is to never pick out your own fruit. Generally, a clerk will assist you and then weigh and price the items. Only when you are sure it is self-service should you pinch a peach and bag it. A weighing station is in the produce section so that you can weigh your purchase and print a price label to attach to the bag.

The second thing you'll notice is that all the deli wares are behind a counter. Never fear, the nice lady with the white hat wants to help you! Just be ready to point to what you want and use the following phrases:

YOU'LL THANK YOURSELF LATER

You don't need to tip your waiter if the service is included. Check the menu for the phrase *Bedienung inbegriffen*.

Etwas davon = Some of that

Wieviel? = How much?

Zwei Pfund = two pounds

Ein halbes Pfund = a half pound

Ein viertel Pfund = a quarter pound

ein Bißchen = a little bit

genug = enough

mehr = more

weniger = less

In Scheiben = sliced

Am Stück = in one piece

Ist das alles? = Is that all?

Das ist alles = That's all

Note that although the metric system is the basis for all measurements in Europe, a pound is commonly used in cooking. (A metric pound is 500 grams, slightly more than an American pound.) Because the unit is familiar to you, use it for the easiest results.

Also note that once you make it to the cashier, you are not quite home free. In Europe, customers bag their own groceries and pay extra for the bags. Make sure you don't hold up the line!

Likes and Wants

Once you find an eatery, it's time to order. Remember that in the German world, lunch is traditionally the largest meal of the day, and dinner is a simpler affair.

Are you ready to tell the waiter what you'd like? Or would you like his recommendation?

Saying what you like is easy with *haben + gern* (to like):

Ich habe gern Fisch. (I like fish.)

Sie hat gern Wurst. (She likes sausage.)

You can also use *gern* with other verbs, such as:

essen = to eat

trinken = to drink

For example:

Ich esse gern. (I like to eat.)
Er trinkt gern. (He likes to drink.)

Now that you've expressed what you like, ask what the waiter would recommend. This is often the best way to find a local specialty.

Was empfehlen Sie? (What do you recommend?)

He'll likely respond with the best choice for the day:

Ich empfehle den Fisch. (I recommend the fish.)

If you would like to order it, get fancy and use the subjunctive mood. The subjunctive mood is the most polite way to ask for what you want, because it express es a condition to be fulfilled. In English, the subjunctive mood is expressed by "would like to have."

The present subjunctive of *haben* is conjugated as follows:

A COMPLETE WASTE OF TIME

When eating out in Germany, it's a complete waste of time to expect:

1. Your soft drink to be large and to contain ice.

2. There to be a non-smoking section.

3. To find booster seats for children.

	Singular	Plural
First person	ich hätte	wir hätten
Second person (informal)	du hättest	ihr hättet
Second person (formal)	Sie hätten	
Third person	er, sie, es hätte	sie hätten

Now you are ready to ask for what you would like:

Ich hätte gern den Fisch. (I would like to have the fish.)

Sie hätte gern die Wurst. (She would like the sausage.)

TOOLS OF THE TRADE

Not since the Middle Ages have diners attacked their plates without the proper tools for the job. You'll be able to ask for any of the necessary items if you learn the following basics:

das Besteck = flatware

der Teller = plate

der Löffel = spoon

das Messer = knife

die Gabel = fork

die Tasse = cup

das Glas = glass

die Rechnung = check, bill

die Serviette = napkin

die Speisekarte = menu

Pretty Please!

You can easily ask for something by using the old "missing item + please" trick. Don't think that you always have

to communicate in complete sentences in a foreign language. Try shouting out to the help, *Die Rechnung, bitte!*, and you'll get what you ask for. It's short and sweet, and it works!

Exercise 2

Try asking for the following items with the "please" trick:

A napkin

_____

A fork

_____

A spoon

_____

A menu

_____

A knife

_____

WHAT TO EAT

I hope you've eaten! You should never go to the grocery store on an empty stomach or learn food vocabulary with a growling tummy. The ingredients in this section will put you on your way to deciphering any menu or filling your shopping cart with confidence.

IF YOU'RE SO
INCLINED

No German breakfast is complete without the use of a *Frühstücksbrett*, a small, wooden cutting board for *Brot* (bread), *Käse* (cheese), and *Schinken* (ham). Buy a small board for each person at your breakfast table and enjoy your morning repast German style. *Guten Morgen!*

Obst und Gemüse (Fruits and Vegetables)

In the summer, German heirloom (old world varieties that don't sacrifice flavor for shelf life) fruits and vegetables make for memorable dining:

Singular	Plural
der Apfel = apple	die Apfel
die Beere = berry	die Beeren
die Birne = pear	die Birnen
die Erbse = pea	die Erbsen
die Gurke = cucumber	die Gurken
die Karotte = carrot	die Karotten
die Kartoffel = potato	die Kartoffeln
der Kirsch = cherry	die Kirschen
der Pilz = mushroom	die Pilze
der Reis = rice	—
die Rosine = raisin	die Rosinen
die Tomate = tomato	die Tomaten
die Zitrone = lemon	die Zitronen
die Zwiebel = onion	die Zwiebeln

Milch und Käse (Milk and Cheese)

The following fresh items in the dairy case will tempt your palate:

die Butter = butter
das Ei = egg/*die Eier*
der Joghurt = yogurt

der Käse = cheese

die Milch = milk

die Sahne = cream

Fleisch und Fisch (Meat and Fish)

You will find that fish is common in northern Germany, whereas pork is common in southern Germany. Beef is available but is often imported.

der Fisch = fish

das Fleisch = meat

die Ente = duck

die Gans = goose

der Herring = herring

das Huhn = chicken

der Kabeljau = cod

der Lachs = salmon

das Rindfleisch = beef

der Schinken = ham

das Schweinefleish = pork

die Shrimps = shrimp

die Wurst = sausage

Getränke (Drinks)

Quench your thirst with the following:

die heiße Schokolade = hot chocolate

der Kaffee = coffee

IF YOU'RE SO INCLINED

If you are a sausage fan, Germany is the destination for you. It's clearly where the 'Wurst is the best! Try these varieties:

die Blutwurst = blood sausage

die Weißwurst = a Bavarian specialty served hot and, properly, only before midday

die Bratwurst = the classic grilled sausage

der Frankfurter = the classic original hot dog

der Nürnberger = a delicious fried sausage, which is sometimes served rolled like a lollipop *der Tee* = tea

das Bier = beer

die Cola = cola

das Mineralwasser = mineral water

der Saft = juice

Der Schnaps = schnapps

der Wein = wine

Gänge (Courses)

The menu in German restaurants is divided into the following logical units:

die Vorspeise = appetizer

das Hauptgericht = main course

die Suppe = soup

der Salat = salad

der Nachtisch = dessert

Practical Practice

Now that you have a handle on German food words, it's time to use them. Make a list of the groceries in your fridge, or make up a list of items that should be in your fridge:

_____   _____

_____   _____

_____   _____

_____   _____

_____   _____

Special Requests

It is hard enough to stick to a normal diet when traveling, let alone special dietary needs. If you have any particular needs, you will want to learn the phrases that apply to your situation. Can't take it? Then leave it! The verb *vertragen* (to tolerate digestively) enables you to make it clear that you have a real reason not to clean your plate.

> *Ich bin vegetarisch.* (I am a vegetarian.)
>
> *Ich bin zuckerkrank.* (I am diabetic.)
>
> *Ich bin auf Diät.* (I am on a diet.)
>
> *Ich vertrage keine Milch.* (I am lactose intolerant.)
>
> *Ich vertrage keine Meeresfrüchte.* (I cannot eat shellfish.)
>
> *Ich vertrage keine Erdnüße.* (I cannot eat peanuts.)

It's in the Details

Because of their common roots, the names of many spices and herbs are the same or similar in English and in German. The following list of the most commonly requested condiments and seasonings highlights the flavors you are likely to encounter in the German cuisine:

> *die Butter* = butter
>
> *der Knoblauch* = garlic
>
> *das Kümmel* = caraway
>
> *die Marmelade* = jam
>
> *der Muskat* = nutmeg

A COMPLETE WASTE OF TIME

Don't expect to find many good vegetarian restaurants during your travels in Europe. If the thought of traditional sausage and headcheese makes you blanch, opt for one of these typical entrees:

1. Find an ethnic restaurant. Chinese or Indian dishes are a good choice.

2. Noodle dishes, such as *Spätzle* (small dumplings) or *Semmelknödel* (large dumplings), make satisfying dinners.

3. *Spargel* (asparagus, particularly the white variety) is a tasty early spring specialty eaten as a main course and served in a variety of ways.

die Nelken = cloves

der Pfeffer = pepper

das Salz = salt

der Senf = mustard

der Zimt = cinnamon

Exercise 3

Remember the old "please" trick from earlier in this chapter? You are ready for the next variation on that theme. The names of food are often referred to as "non-count nouns," which are things that cannot be counted, such as milk, pepper, or love. To use the "please" trick, simply omit the article and ask for *Butter, bitte!*

Try asking for the following non-count items with the "please" trick:

Bread

_____

Water

_____

Salt

_____

Beer

_____

Milk

_____

One way to keep your need to talk to a minimum is to go to a buffet restaurant. You'll get exactly what you want with a minimum of communication. Your worst problem will be making sure your eyes aren't bigger than your stomach.

My Compliments to the Chef

Expressions of praise will get you further in life than insults. Learn the following terms and be ready to compliment anything, anywhere:

ausgezeichnet = exceptional

fantastisch – fantastic

wunderbar = wonderful

vorzüglich = excellent

Praise the chef like this and you might get a private tour of the kitchen or a recipe to take home with you:

Das Fleisch war wunderbar! (The meat was wonderful!)

Der Nachtisch war vorzüglich! (The dessert was excellent!)

MENU PLANNING

The best way to most peoples' memories is through their stomachs! Why not plan an authentic German meal? Before you make excuses about not having enough chairs for guests, remember you can plan a pretend dinner (complete with ice sculptures) or make it easy on your dishwasher by eating out.

IF YOU'RE SO INCLINED

Combine fresh air with German culture. Enjoy your next beer outdoors with a plate of radishes and salt. (A large spiral-cut daikon radish is most authentically German.) If you like, make a summertime classic: a Radler (half lemon-lime soda and half beer). Add some pretzels and you're celebrating summer the German way!

For inspiration, look for recipes in German cookbooks from the library or your local bookstore. If you are lucky enough to have a German restaurant close by, call and ask for a copy of the menu. Here are some classic main dishes you may want to try:

- *Bauernplatte:* A farmer's platter featuring a little bit of every meat (not for the weak of heart)
- *Jägerschnitzel:* A cutlet in mushroom sauce
- *Hasenpfeffer:* Seasoned stew of rabbit
- *Käsespätzle:* Dumplings backed with cheese
- *Kassler Rippchen:* A uniquely German dish of smoked pork loin
- *Rolladen:* Rolled beef filled with cabbage, pickle, and bacon
- *Sauerbraten:* A classic dish of marinated beef in ginger gravy

Serious Sides

German side dishes are just as hearty as the meat they accompany. Be ready to take carbohydrates to new heights with the following:

- *Blaukraut:* Red cabbage served warm and tangy
- *Kartoffelpuffer:* Potato pancakes
- *Kartoffelpüree:* Mashed potatoes
- *Kartoffelsalat:* Potato salad served deliciously warm and with bacon
- *Knödel:* Large dumplings made of bread or potatoes
- *Spätzle:* Little dumplings similar to homemade pasta

Delicious Desserts

Dessert is always a highlight. If the following don't motivate you to try a German dinner, nothing will:

- **Apfelstrudel:** Apple strudel
- **Rote Grütze:** A berry compote served with vanilla sauce
- **Schwarzwälder Kirschtorte:** A Black Forest cake made with chocolate, cherries, and cream

You can find recipes in German magazines at larger newsstands. Plan your menu in as much detail as you can. Even if you don't actually go through with it, it can be fun to pretend.

You can use the following template to create a handwritten menu for your guests. Simply insert the dishes of your choice. Fräulein Manners would be proud!

Ein Deutscher Abend
(A German Evening)

Aperitif/Aperitif

Vorspeise/Appetizer

Wein/Wine

Suppe/Soup

Hauptgericht/Main Course

Gemüse/Vegetable

Salat/Salad

Nachtisch/Dessert

Now all that's left to do is to set the table and light the candles. Before you break bread, you might want to say the following old-fashioned, simple German grace:

Komm lieber Herr Jesus, sei unser Gast,
und segne, was Du uns bescheret hast.

(Come, Jesus, be our guest,
and bless what you have given in our trust.)

If you are in the mood for a silly saying, try this:

Piep, piep, piep,
wir hab'n uns alle lieb,
jeder esse, was er kann,
nur nicht seinen Nebenmann.
Guten Appetit!

(Peep, peep, peep,
We each other well keep,
Each eat what he can,
Just not his neighbor man.)

Well, this is one chapter that should leave you wanting more—more to eat, that is! What's for dinner at your house tonight?

Beyond Birkenstocks: Shopping and Fashion

German fashion seems to be a world of extremes, from the clumsiness of sturdy, healthy sandals to the sharp, cold lines of modern black and white designs and the somewhat gnome-looking traditional fashions of the Black Forest and Bavaria. You don't have to be a fashion victim, however; you can express yourself in German and take it or leave it. In this chapter, you'll discover the skills you need to confidently shop until you drop.

HELPING AND VERBS WITH DATIVE OBJECTS

Anticipation is the name of the lazy shopping game. Knowing what you will be asked is half the battle. Upon entering a store, you will most likely hear the following phrase:

> *Guten Tag! Kann ich Ihnen helfen?* (Good day! Can I help you?)

Notice that the verb *helfen* takes a dative object, in this case *Ihnen*. Don't let this fluster you; some verbs require dative objects. Among them are the following:

jemandem helfen = to help someone

jemandem gefallen = to like

jemandem passen = to fit

jemandem stehen = to suit

The dative pronouns are as follows:

	Singular	Plural
First person	mir	uns
Second person	dir	euch
Second person (formal)	Ihnen	
Third person	ihm, ihr	ihnen

Look at the following examples, and you can see how useful verbs that take dative objects can be:

Das gefällt mir. (I like that.)

Das paßt mir. (That fits me.)

Das steht mir. (That suits me.)

Das hilft mir. (That helps me.)

Exercise 1

Time to practice! Translate the following sentences to ready yourself for wardrobe warfare (For example: Can you help me? *Können Sie mir helfen?*)

That fits you.

_____

Do you like that?

_____

We like that.

_____

That suits her.

_____

That fits him.

_____

LOOKING—REFLEXIVE ACTIVITIES

When you're just looking around, say, _Ich schaue mich nur um_. That leads to the next topic: reflexive verbs. Reflexive verbs reflect the action of the verb in the subject. In English, you are familiar with the example of "I wash myself." German, however, has many other instances in which a verb is reflexive.

Here are some of the most useful reflexive verbs:

sich bedienen = to help one's self

sich waschen = to wash one's self

sich umschauen = to look around (Note: _um_ is a separable prefix)

sich anziehen = to dress (Note: _an_ is a separable prefix)

QUICK ⟨🔳⟩ PAINLESS

The formal pronouns (Sie, Ihnen) are always capitalized. The informal pronoun is also capitalized in correspondence to that person (du, dir, and so on) as a sign of polite respect.

There are other separable prefix verbs, such as *aufstehen* (to get up), that are not reflexive. For example: *Ich stehe auf.* (I get up.) Although there is no simple way of knowing which verbs have separable prefixes —sorry, you'll just have to memorize them—you can take comfort in the fact they usually are words of direction, such as: up, to, until.

Simple Separable Prefixes

Some reflexive verbs have separable prefixes. That is, the prefix is moved to the end of the sentence. For example: when the reflexive verb is used in a sentence such as "*Wir schauen uns um*" (*sich umschauen*). When the verb is used in the present tense, the *um* goes to the end of the sentence.

Reflexive Pronouns

There is no trick to knowing which verbs are reflexive; you just have to memorize them. You will be relieved, however, that the reflexive pronouns will seem very familiar to you (with the exception of *sich*).

	Singular	Plural
First person	mich	uns
Second person (informal)	dich	euch
Second person (formal)	Sich	
Third person	sich	sich

Note that only the formal pronoun is capitalized.

Exercise 2

Again, it will take some practice to get used to this new way of working with verbs. Here's an exercise to get you up to speed.

Translate the following phrases. (For example: I get dressed. *Ich ziehe mich an.*)

I am looking around.

_____

You are getting dressed.

_____

He is helping himself.

_____

We are washing ourselves.

_____

She is getting dressed.

_____

WHAT'S IN STORE: CLOTHING AND SOUVENIRS

No doubt you'll wander into a few stores during your European adventure. Whether you are shopping for something specific to expand your travel wardrobe or for a few souvenirs to take back home, you'll want to be able to ask for certain items and how much they cost.

The Bottom Line

When you are ready to put down your money, the most important phrase you can know is:

Wieviel kostet das? (How much does that cost?)

The verb *kosten* (to cost) is a regular verb. It is also a cognate of the English word "cost," so at least one part of paying won't be too painful.

The Goods

Stores in Europe tend to be much more specialized than the American one-stop-shopping megastores. Don't be

QUICK 🔳 *PAINLESS*

One of the least expensive ways to shop is with your eyes. Browsing is acceptable, just say *Ich schaue mich nur um.* (I'm just looking). Your memories will be your best souvenirs. And you'll still be able to close your suitcase!

surprised to find stores that sell only buttons, socks, or scarves, for example. Because of this specialization, the clerks know their wares very well. Here are some of the words you'll need to find the stores you want:

> *der Apotheke* = pharmacy (for prescription and over-the-counter medications)
>
> *das Blumengeschäft* = flower shop
>
> *der Buchladen* = bookstore
>
> *die Drogerie* = drugstore (specializing in cosmetics)
>
> *das Geschäft* = shop
>
> *der Geschenkladen* = gift shop
>
> *das Kaufhaus* = department store
>
> *der Laden* = store
>
> *das Modegeschäft* = clothing store
>
> *das Musikgeschäft* = music store
>
> *das Spielwarengeschäft* = toy store

Souvenir Savvy

Shelves around the world are adorned with souvenirs from Europe. You can continue the tradition by dutifully shopping for the classic items that scream "I've been there and done that." Or you can break from the mold and bring back German kitchen utensils or whatever odd items catch your eye. Here are the classics to get you started:

> *der Bierkrug* = beer stein
>
> *die Hummelfigur* = Hummel figurine

IF YOU'RE SO INCLINED

Paris isn't the only European capital with fabulous flea markets. Check out the *Flohmarkt* in Berlin or Vienna. These outdoor markets can be a great place to find inexpensive, authentic souvenirs. They are often open on Sundays, unlike most other stores, and give you a great chance to practice your German while bartering with the locals.

die Kuckucksuhr = cuckoo clock

die Postkarte = postcard

das Taschenmesser = pocket knife

die Uhr = watch

This list is meant only to get you started. Whatever your interest, you'll find a remembrance suitable for you.

Exercise 3

Ready to ask for what you want? If you want a watch, for example, say *Ich möchte eine Uhr*. Use this pattern to ask for the following items:

A cuckoo clock

_____

A postcard

_____

A beer stein

_____

A pocket knife

_____

Wardrobe Workhorses

For the practically inclined, clothing makes a great souvenir. There are even regional styles such as the *Dirndl* skirt, or *Lodenjacke*—a warm jacket made of felt-like woolen cloth. With the following words for articles of clothing, you'll be ready to get some serious shopping under your belt:

der Anzug = men's suit

der Badeanzug = bathing suit

die Bluse = blouse

der Gürtel = belt

das Hemd = shirt

das Kleid = dress

die Handschuhe = gloves (literally, hand shoes)

die Hose = pants

der Hut = hat

die Jacke = jacket

die Jeans = jeans

das Kostüm = women's suit

die Krawatte = tie

der Mantel = coat

der Pulli = sweater

der Rock = skirt

der Sakko = blazer

die Sandalen = sandals

der Schal = scarf

der Schlafanzug = pajamas

die Shorts = shorts

die Socken = socks

die Strumpfhose = panty hose

das T-shirt = T-shirt

die Unterwäsche = underwear

Dressing for the Black Forest

Hiking is a passion in Germany. Most people dress a bit like gnomes in preparation for the event. If you want to get along with the natives, you better take it seriously. Unleash your *Wanderlust* with a hiking stick in hand. Add a rucksack and a light lunch, wear as much green and gray as possible, and perhaps highlight your muscular lower legs with red socks and sturdy walking shoes. You'll be able to get anything you might have forgotten at a sporting goods store. Now you're ready to wander with the best of them.

Hike Your Way Through Europe

Can you walk and talk at the same time? You'll want to know the following vocabulary if you can:

bergauf = up hill

bergrunter = down hill

die Blase = blister

der Rucksack = rucksack

das Sportgeschäft = sporting goods store

steil = steep

die Wanderkarte = hiking map

die Wanderschuhe = hiking shoes

der Wanderstock = hiking stick

der Wanderweg = hiking trail

Wie weit noch? = How much farther?

IF YOU'RE SO INCLINED

Germans are particular about the health of their feet; sandals are a must at public baths, pools, and saunas. Whether you plan to travel in Germany or enjoy your new German skills at home, pick up a cheap pair of sandals and get into German *Fußkultur*. While you're at it, treat yourself to a medicated *Fußbad*, too.

Material Matters

It's a material world. It matters to most of us whether an item is 100 percent polyester or 100 percent cotton. To express fiber content, use the phrase *aus + material*. For example: *Das Hemd ist aus Baumwolle.* (The shirt is made of cotton.) Here is the run-down on fabrics:

die Baumwolle = cotton (literally, tree wool)

die Kunstfaser = artificial fiber

das Leder = leather

die Seide = silk

die Viskose = rayon

die Wolle = wool

Exercise 4

Translate the following sentences and get ready to dress in style:

The scarf is made of silk.

_____

The hat is made of wool.

_____

The jacket is made of leather.

_____

The pants are made of cotton.

_____

The dress is made of rayon.

_____

Wearing and Buying Her, Him, and It

She is my favorite jacket. What? Are you wearing a living female mink? No, but that's the way German works. If you talk about any noun, you need to take it/her/his gender into consideration when you talk about it/him/her. I'll show you what this means using the verbs *tragen* (to wear) and *kaufen* (to buy).

Tragen (to wear) is a strong verb. Notice that it takes an umlaut in the second and third person singular. (For a review on how verbs are conjugated, see Chapter 9, "Do It in German: Having Your Way with Verbs.")

A COMPLETE WASTE OF TIME

Welcome to the "Old World!" Don't expect the same level of customer service and convenience while shopping in Europe.

1. Never expect stores to be open on Sunday or even after noon on Saturday.

2. Don't wait until the evening to go shopping; generally, stores close at six o'clock.

3. Don't wait for help to come to you. Stand up for your right to shop and say, *Entschuldigen Sie, bitte!* (Excuse me, please.)

Tragen (to wear)	Singular	Plural
First person	ich trage	wir tragen
Second person (informal)	du trägst	ihr tragt
Second person (formal)	Sie tragen	
Third person	er, sie, es trägt	sie tragen

Another verb you'll often want is the regular verb *kaufen* (to buy):

Kaufen (to buy)	Singular	Plural
First person	ich kaufe	wir kaufen
Second person (formal)	du kaufst	ihr kauft
Second person (formal)	Sie kaufen	
Third person	er, sie, es kauft	sie kaufen

When you are talking about a feminine noun, for example, *die Jacke*, you must say you wear it, using the pronoun that expresses the noun's gender. Here are some examples:

Object	Sentence with Pronoun
die Jacke	Ich kaufe sie.
der Hut	Ich trage ihn.
das Hemd	Ich trage es.

Exercise 5

It takes some getting used to for English speakers to feel comfortable referring to what one thinks of as an "it" as a "he" or "she." See if you can fill in the following blanks with the correct form of the pronoun. (For example: Ich kaufe den Anzug. Ich trage *ihn*.):

1. Ich kaufe die Jacke. Ich trage _____.

2. Wir kaufen die Schuhe. Wir tragen _____.

3. Sie kauft das Hemd. Sie trägt _____.

4. Er kauft den Schal. Er trägt _____.

5. Du kaufst den Hut. Du trägst _____.

Sizing It Up

You'll save a lot of time in the dressing room if you know your German size from the start.

Use the following tables to compare some typical American sizes with their German counterparts:

Men's Suits

United States	36	38	40	42	44	46	48
Germany		46	48	50	52	54	56	58

Dress Sizes

United States	6	8	10	12	14	16
Germany	34	36	38	40	42	44

Men's Shoes

United States	8	8.5	9.5	10.5	11.5	12
Germany	41	42	43	44	45	46

Women's Shoes

United States	6	6.5	7	7.5	8	8.5	9
Germany	36	37	38	39	40	41	42

Not Quite Right?

Even with the right size, some things might not fit. Remember to use the proper pronoun for the gender of the noun you are using.

The following examples give you all the options you'll need to describe *ein Hemd* (a shirt) or any other item that really isn't you:

Es ist zu groß. (It is too big.)

Es ist zu klein. (It is too small.)

Es ist zu dunkel. (It is too dark.)

Es ist zu hell. (It is too light.)

Es ist zu kurz. (It is too short.)

Es ist zu lang. (It is too long.)

Es ist zu deutsch. (It is too German.)

DM Discounts

Sales in Europe are highly predictable. You'll be very lucky if you are shopping during the end-of-season clearance sale (*Schlußverkauf*). Generally, these sales are scheduled at the end of the summer and winter seasons. In fact, clearance sale dates must be approved by the government. Nonetheless, it can't hurt to ask whether anything is on sale. For example: *Haben Sie etwas im Sonderangebot?* (Do you have anything on sale?)

THE EURO

With the coming of the Euro—the standard currency for all of the European Union (EU)—German and Austrian denominations will be a thing of the past as of January 1, 2002. On that date, bills and coins will be issued in the Euro currency. The Euro is already in use for cashless transactions.

Money Talks

Prices are the most common of all numbers you will deal with when traveling. Here are two more key words you'll need to know when it comes to paying for all the fun (revisit Chapter 11, "Gute Mannieren: Poise and Politeness for All Occasions," to review money terms you've already learned):

   der Preis = price

   die MWS (Mehrwertsteuer) = Value-added tax (a consumption tax that non-EU residents can have refunded upon exiting the country; ask the salesperson for details)

Look in the financial section of today's newspaper (or go online) to find the exchange rates for the countries you will be visiting:

$1 = _____ DM

$1 = _____ CHF

$1 = _____ AUS

Pretend you are going shopping in Europe. Estimate the price you would pay in dollars for the following items. Then use the rates you researched to convert to local currency and fill in the approximate prices.

	In Germany	In Switzerland	In Austria
ein Pullover aus Wolle			
ein Kuckucksuhr			
ein Schal aus Seide			
eine Lodenjacke			
eine Wanderkarte			

Now that you are ready to shop in Europe, it would be very nice of you to ask your friends and family what they want from your trip to the German-speaking world. You can always mail home the stuff that won't fit in your suitcase.

From Alpine Castles to Checkpoint Charlie: Sightseeing

Whether you are an armchair traveler or a frequent-flyer mile-earning jet setter, it's likely that one of the reasons you are interested in learning German is to learn about the sights. Whatever your interests—from medieval torture chambers to Bauhaus architecture, from model trains to Alpine lakes—you'll find an interesting way to spend time while in the German-speaking world. To make certain you can find your way into, around, and back out of all the attractions, this chapter focuses on the finer points of prepositions. And what trip to Europe would be complete without a discussion of the weather? You'll also get a short course on the abbreviations you'll see on signs and in travel literature. Finally, for an adventure closer to home, you'll get an overview of the history of Germans in the United States.

SEEING THE SIGHTS

You're armed with a guidebook or map of the local sights and are wearing your most comfortable shoes. It's time to embark on your initial adventure. Walking is the best way to see the sights of European cities. Wander your way down a cobblestone street or up an Alpine trail. Keep your eyes open for signs pointing out the following attractions:

die Ausstellung = exhibit

der Berg = mountain

die Brücke = bridge

die Burg = castle

der Dom = cathedral

die Fabrik = factory

das Fachwerkhaus = half-timbered building

der Fluß = river

die Fußgängerzone = pedestrian area

die Grenze = national border

die Insel = island

die Kathedrale = cathedral

das Kino = movie theater

die Kirche = church

das Konzert = concert

der Kurort = spa

der Markt = market

die Mauer = the Wall

Make the countdown to your trip informational and scenic. Buy a calendar featuring scenes from your favorite German destinations or load a screensaver with a map or destination. Vary the image with the season as you cross off the days from your calendar.

The Lazy Way

die Messe = trade show

das Museum = museum

das Schloss = castle

der See = lake

der Strand = beach

das Theater = theater

der Turm = tower

der Wald = forest

der Weinberg = vineyard

der Zoo = zoo

Just Looking

You'll want to take in as much with your eyes (or your camera) as you can during your wanderings, so the verb *sehen* (to see) will be very useful. *Sehen* is a strong verb, which means its stem changes in the second person plural and singular and in the third person singular.

Sehen (to see)	Singular	Plural
First person	ich sehe	wir sehen
Second person (informal)	du siehst	ihr sieht
Second person (formal)	Sie sehen	
Third person	er sie es sieht	sie sehen

Ready to do some sight seeing?

Sehen Sie die Kirche? (Do you see the church?)

Ich sehe den Berg, den See, und die Brücke. (I see the mountain, the lake, and the bridge.)

A COMPLETE WASTE OF TIME

The worst things you can do when heading off on your own grand tour are:

1. Try to see all of German-speaking Europe in a week. Allow yourself time to enjoy, or reduce your itinerary.

2. Forget your international student ID card for discounts to museums, theaters, and concerts.

3. Pack too much. You can buy almost anything once you arrive if you still really need it.

Exercise 1

You're walking through the German countryside and come across a castle above a lake near a forest. There is a tower near the castle, and an island in the lake. You want to write a postcard to a friend describing the scene. Use this space to write that postcard:

_____

_____

_____

_____

Itinerary Items

You should plan your visit with an eye to the clock and calendar. Here are the words you'll need to get your itinerary in place:

am Abend = in the evening

gestern = yesterday

heute = today

am Montag = on Monday

am Morgen = in the morning

morgen = tomorrow

am Nachmittag = in the afternoon

diese Woche = this week

nächste Woche = next week

um zehn Uhr = at ten o'clock

QUICK ■■ PAINLESS

Some museums are free on Sundays. Check the local newspapers and city magazines for the current exhibits!

Ready to plan your day? Remember that if anything comes before the subject in the sentence, the verb and subject are inverted. For example:

Wir sehen die Kirche heute. (We see the church today.)

Heute sehen wir die Kirche. (Today we see the church.)

PREPOSITIONAL PROPOSITION

Prepositions are useful little words. They tell us where, when, and how things are done. It is no surprise to English speakers that every preposition must have an object. (Remember how you are not supposed to end a sentence with a preposition? Well, that's because it needs an object following it.) What is new for native speakers of English is that German prepositions use objects in different cases. Some prepositions can be used only with one case or another, whereas other prepositions can be used with more than one case and have more than one meaning.

Dative Prepositions

The following prepositions are used only with dative objects:

aus = out of, from

außer = except

bei = by, near, with, at

mit = with

nach = after, to

seit = since

von = from, of

zu = to

Notice that the prepositions in the following sentences use the dative case for their objects:

Ich gehe aus dem Schloss. (I go out of the castle.)

Ich esse alles außer der Wurst. (I eat everything except the sausage.)

Das Museum bei dem See ist sehr schön. (The museum by the lake is very lovely.)

Exercise 2

Try your hand at dative prepositions by translating the following sentences into English:

Wir essen in dem Cafe.

_____

Der See mit der Insel ist sehr schön.

_____

Nach dem Konzert gehen wir nach Stuttgart.

_____

Von dem Hotel ist es zwei Kilometer.

_____

Seit dem Abend bin ich in Österreich.

_____

Accusative Prepositions

The following prepositions always use the accusative case:

bis = until, as far as

durch = through

für = for

gegen = against

ohne = without

um = around, about

The following sentences show the accusative objects of prepositions:

Ich sehe bis dem See. (I see as far as the lake.)

Wir gehen durch den Wald. (We go through the forest.)

Wir fahren um die Stadt. (We drive around the city.)

Exercise 3

Translate the following phrases to practice using prepositions that require the accusative case:

The mountain without the castle

_____

Through the river

_____

Around the forest

_____

IF YOU'RE SO INCLINED

Most German cities feature a pedestrian area known as *die Fußgängerzone*. This compound noun literally translates as a "foot-goer zone." You'll find that a lot of attractions have compound nouns for names. The words you have learned appear to be combined into one long word. Don't be afraid of it; break it down into its elements and you can decipher the name by its context. Try your hand at these: *Bergsee, Schlossmuseum,* and *Waldkirche*.

For the museum

_____

Until the concert

_____

Accusative/Dative Prepositions

Some prepositions can use either the dative case or the accusative case. Generally, the dative case is used for expressing a fixed location, whereas the accusative case is used for expressing motion to a location.

The following prepositions can use both the accusative and dative cases:

an = at, on, to, up to

auf = upon, on, to

hinter = behind

in = in, into

neben = beside

über = above, over

unter = under

vor = before, in front of

zwischen = between

You can see the difference in action between the dative and the accusative cases.

Dative (at a fixed location):
Ich bin über dem Haus. (I am above the house.)

Accusative (motion to a location):
Ich gehe über das Haus. (I go above the house.)

Knowing when to use the accusative case versus the dative case takes some practice, but you will soon get the hang of it. Just remember that dative prepositions stay in "dat" place and accusative prepositions say "'scuse me" as they go off on their way.

Exercise 4

Translate the following sentences:

I go in the church.

_____

I am in the church.

_____

We are under the bridge.

_____

We go under the bridge.

_____

Get into Contractions

The following contractions are used when the prepositions an and in come together with dem. Unlike contractions in English, these are not optional:

an + dem = am

in + dem = im

WEATHERING THE STORM

The weather plays a big role in helping you decide what to see when traveling. Museums are great refuges from the heat or cold. Warm, sunny days call for outdoor

IF YOU'RE SO
INCLINED

With the help of some desk toys—cars, plastic dinosaurs, nifty paperweights, and so on—you can test your understanding of the difference between the accusative and dative. For example: "Is the dinosaur *in* the car (dative) or getting *into* (accusative) the car?" (This is best done out of sight of the boss!)

Use public transporta-
tion in the bigger cities.
You'll see more of the
town's real people than
you would in a cab.
Plus, it is inexpensive
and easy to use.

excursions to mountain lakes. What Europe lacks during gray winter days it makes up for with the warm days of summer. Just learn to dress for the prevailing conditions. Travel during the transitional seasons of spring and fall can be full of surprises, so pack for the worst and hope for the best.

The weather is also a good conversation starter. You will be ready to open a weather station once you have mastered the following phrases:

Wie ist das Wetter? (How's the weather?)

Es ist schön! (It is lovely!)

Das Wetter ist schlecht. (The weather is bad.)

Das Wetter ist fantastisch. (The weather is fantastic.)

The weather in Europe never knows a dull moment; at some point you'll probably encounter the following terms:

bewölkt = cloudy

böhig = gusty

frisch = fresh, chilly

heiß = hot

heiter = clear

kalt = cold

kühl = cool

mäßig = moderate

nebelig = foggy

regnerisch = rainy

schlecht = bad

schön = lovely

stürmisch = stormy

warm = warm

wechselhaft = changeable

windig = windy

It also doesn't hurt to memorize the four seasons—not Vivaldi's score, the German ones.

der Herbst = fall

der Winter = winter

der Frühling = spring

der Sommer = summer

And don't forget about the weather—come rain or shine:

der Blitz = lightning

der Donner = thunder

der Hagel = hail

der Himmel = sky

der Nebel = fog

der Regen = rain

der Schnee = snow

die Sonne = sun

die Überschwemmung = flood

Try your hand at being a weather watcher. Describe how you perceive the seasons. For example: *Das Wetter im Frühling ist wechselhaft mit Regen und Sonne. Es ist auch windig und kühl.*

Exercise Five

Das Wetter im Winter ist

_____

_____

_____

Das Wetter im Sommer ist

_____

_____

_____

QUICK  PAINLESS

Note that the seasons are masculine in German.

While driving on the Autobahn, you might be surprised to have your radio program frequently (incessantly, it seems) interrupted by a strange tone followed by traffic advisories. You can also tune your radio to weather forecasts. Both tend to be short and repetitive, so treat them like mini language lessons.

Take Your Temperature

You can tell the temperature by looking at what people are wearing, but you'll know better what to wear if you know the temperature before you head out. Remember that all of Europe uses degrees Celsius to track the mercury. Here are some useful phrases to know:

> *Was ist die Temperatur?* (What is the temperature?)
>
> *Es hat zehn Grad.* (It is ten degrees.)
>
> *Es hat minus fünf Grad.* (It is five degrees below.)

ABBREVIATION BREVITY

With all the long words in German, it's no wonder abbreviations are so popular. Don't be left in the cold by the code. Maps and signs in Europe use abbreviations extensively. The following are some of the most common abbreviations you'll encounter along your trip:

Abbreviation	German	English
A	Autobahn	Freeway
AG	Aktiengesellschaft	Stock corporation
B	Bundesstraße	Federal highway
Bhf.	Bahnhof	Train station
EG	Erdgeschoß	Ground floor
D	Damen	Ladies
H	Herren	Men
PLZ	Postleitzahl	Postal code

S	Straßenbahn	Streetcar
Str.	Straße	Street
U	U-bahn	Subway
z.B.	zum Beispiel	For example

For even more abbreviations, check the back of a good German dictionary. (And for more about good German dictionaries, see Appendix B, "If You Really Want More, Read These.")

DISCOVERING GERMANS IN AMERIKA

Germans are very aware of their history, and they often like to remind Americans that our history is oh-so-short. But the history of Germans in America is part of both cultures, and learning about it is a great way to understand both the German people and how they have contributed to American culture.

Most American cities have taken in German immigrants. There are many reminders of this common history. German is spoken in cities in Pennsylvania, Texas, and Minnesota, for example. Oregon is home of Mount Angel, a German monastery. Cities such as Milwaukee, Detroit, Pittsburgh, and Oakland still have German *Turnvereine* (sport clubs) and *Sängerbünde* (singing clubs). Take a trip to your local German restaurant for a German-language newspaper, which will lead you to other clubs and institutions.

You can also visit your local library or historical society to learn more about Germans in your area. You will

IF YOU'RE SO
INCLINED

Meteorologically minded folks may want to memorize the conversion for Fahrenheit into Celsius: Subtract 32 from the Fahrenheit number, then multiply by .5.

To convert from Celsius to Fahrenheit, multiply the Celsius number by 1.8 and add 32.

QUICK ⬤ PAINLESS

You don't have to look like a tourist to take a mini-vacation *mit deutschem Stil*. See the sights like a German would! One option is to wear sandals with dark socks and shorts. Take a trip to the local spa or view your own city with a *Baedecker* guide in hand. Visit with both wonder and a critical eye, and you've got it down.

likely find pictures of German immigrants and their cultural institutions. From there you can visit original German neighborhoods and identify German street names or see the German influence in the architecture. A German-theme walking tour is a good activity if you live in or near an older city. If you live in a suburban or rural area, use a map or atlas to locate cities with German names, and then locate original German settlements.

Perhaps genealogy is your interest. You could do some research to ferret out your German ancestry.

Another way to tap into the German-American connection is to look at the American West through the German imagination. The Germans have a long-standing fascination with the Wild West; they helped to settle it. The German landscape painter, Albert Bierstadt, produced some of the most significant landscape paintings of the American West, as well as portraits of its native people. Purchase or borrow a catalog of his paintings and spend some time reliving the wonder he felt in this immense, magnificent land.

Finally, you may want to check out the fictionalized portrayal of the American West in one of the many books by Karl May. His *Winnitou* novels are a good place to start. They are available in both German and English. You can get a free preview online at http://gutenberg. aol.de/autoren/frames/may.htm). His accounts are clearly romanticized, but they have indelibly shaped the German understanding of the West and their view of Americans and our history.

The next time a German laments, "You Americans have no history," gently remind him or her that Germany's history is part of our history too! In fact, a very narrow vote back in Benjamin Franklin's day ended in English being declared the national language over German. Had things gone a little differently, you might now be reading a book called *Learn English The Lazy Way*.

Chapter sixteen

Guten Tag!
Pleasant Conversation

Conversations with people on the street or in a train compartment can add a lot of fun to your trip. They can also enrich your relationship with your German business partners or extended family. In this chapter, you will explore how to use what you already know to get the ball rolling.

In this modern world, you need to learn a few tricks for using the telephone and know what to expect in real-life conversations. And to make sure you get enough practice, I'll give you a role-playing activity to get your creative juices flowing.

GETTING STARTED

What's in a name? A lot! You'll need to ask the following question frequently as you navigate through foreign lands and meet people. Learn the answer, and you'll make new friends.

Wie heißen Sie? (What is your name?)

Ich heiße Karen Smith. (My name is Karen Smith.)

The verb *heißen* (to be called) is regular, but because it ends in *ß*, no *s* is added in the second person singular ending.

Heißen (to be called)	Singular	Plural
First person	ich heiße	wir heißen
Second person (informal)	du heißt	ihr heißt
Second person (formal)	Sie heißen	
Third person	er, sie, es heißt	sie heißen

There is more than one way to ask for someone's name. To be ready for any possibility, learn the following phrases, too:

Wie ist Ihr Name? (What is your name?)

Mein Name ist Karen Farmer. (My name is Karen Farmer.)

The preceding sentences are as easy to use as those that use *heißen*; simply invert the question and add your name.

Because many names come from Biblical or historical roots, you'll recognize many similarities in German and English names:

German	English
Andreas	Andrew
Anna	Anne
Dörthe	Dorothy

Fritz	Fred
Hans (Johannes)	John
Heinz	well…
Hilde	Hilda
Kristoph	Christopher
Kristiana	Christine
Margarethe	Margaret
Wilhelm	William

If your name is similar to a German standard name, you may want to adopt that pronunciation while traveling to make your life easier. You would appreciate the same courtesy from a foreign visitor, right? Some German names are very foreign to English ears. For example:

Men	**Women**
Berndt	Beate
Jürgen	Dagmar
Lutz	Ute
Uwe	

Regardless whether your name has a German counterpart, adopt a German name for the following exercise in conversation skills. You can be creative and playful in your choice, or more serious. Pick a name that gives you latitude to express yourself freely; that's the point! What do you want to call yourself today? Nice to meet you, or should I say *Angenehm!*

QUICK ⬤ PAINLESS

Remember that in conversations many of the words and structures you'll need for your response are handed to you in the question. Listen carefully for the clues and use your working memory to hold onto them long enough to reply.

When conversing with Germans, you should not:

1. Use the *du* form. Use *Sie* and switch to the familiar form when you are invited to do so.

2. Be surprised if they smile and talk less than Americans. It doesn't mean they aren't friendly.

3. Be surprised if they don't speak "school-book" German. Real-life conversations have a lot of variation and "fill" words. They can give you the time you need to understand what was said.

Anna	*Guten Tag! Ich heiße Anna Schmidt. Wie heißen Sie?* (Good day! My name is Anna Schmidt. What is yours?)
Julia	*Ich heiße Julia Moster. Angenehm! Und wie heißt Ihr Hund?* (My name is Julia Moster. Nice to meet you! And what's your dog's name?)
Anna	*Mein Hund heißt Max. Er hat viel Energie heute.* (My dog's name is Max. He has a lot of energy today.)
Julia	*Das sehe ich. Ich habe auch einen Hund.* (I see that. I have a dog too.)
Anna	*Ja? Dann verstehen Sie.* (Yes? Then you understand.)
Julia	*Auf Wiedersehen.* (Good bye.)

WHENCE AND WHEREFORE

For a good ice-breaker, ask your new German friends where they are from and what they do. People love to talk about themselves, and if you ask the right questions you can get them talking and then sit back and enjoy listening to their responses.

Where Are You From?

German speakers are very familiar with geography. They are likely to know the names of all fifty of the United States. You can start the ball rolling with a discussion of your home. You can tell them what country, state, or city you are from by using the *kommen + aus* form, as follows:

Ich komme aus Amerika. (I am from America.)

Ich komme aus Illinois. (I am from Illinois.)

Ich komme aus Chicago. (I am from Chicago.)

While traveling, you are likely to meet other English speakers from around the world. Notice that the names of the following countries are slightly different in German:

Wir kommen aus Kanada. (We are from Canada.)

Er kommt aus England/Australien/Neuseeland. (He is from England/Australia/New Zealand.)

And remember: It's always polite to ask your new acquaintances where they are from:

Woher kommen Sie? (Where are you from?)

Then, prompt them for more information by asking:

Wie ist es dort? (How is it there?)

Destination please!

Wohin gehen Sie? (Where are you going?)

Now that you've got the hang of asking questions, you might want to delve further. Other useful questions of general interest include:

Wo arbeiten Sie? (Where do you work?)

Ich arbeite bei IBM. (I work for IBM.)

Note that the preposition *bei* is used with company names to indicate where a person works.

IF YOU'RE SO
INCLINED

All German first names must be approved by the court clerk before they can be foisted on innocent babies, which explains the rather monotonous collection of first names you will encounter in Germany. By law a name must reflect the child's sex and protect the child's well-being. Regardless, some names sound odd to English ears. Rest assured that this is also true the other way around!

When Germans want to express the actual physical location of where they live, eat, and go to school or work, they use *in*, as follows:

Wo wohnen Sie? (Where do you live?)

Ich wohne in Hamburg. (I live in Hamburg.)

Wo gehst Du zur Schule? (Where do you go to school?)

Ich gehe zur Schule in München. (I go to school in Munich.)

Other useful answers to what questions include:

Was machen Sie hier? (What are you doing here?)

Ich mache Urlaub. (I am on vacation.)

Ich bin auf Geschäftsreise. (I am on a business trip.)

Ich besuche Freunde. (I am visiting friends.)

TELEFON FÜR HERR SCHMIDT

Talking on the telephone is more of a challenge than talking to someone in person, because you do not have all the visual clues you have in a face-to-face conversation. A good thing about telephone calls, however, is that you are in complete control. When you initiate the call it is you who is going after information. Learn these basic strategies to get to your man and get the answer you need:

Wo ist die nächste Telefonzelle? (Where is the next public telephone?)

An easy-to-use structure in conversations is *Was für einen/ein/eine...?* (What kind of a...?) Any time you want to ask more about someone's response, just grab a word from their answer and add it to the structure. For example: *Ich gehe zur Schule in Hamburg. Was für eine Schule?* (I go to school in Hamburg. What kind of school?)

Darf ich Ihr Telefon benutzen? (May I use your phone?)

Guten Tag! Darf ich Frau Mayer sprechen? (Hello. May I speak to Ms. Mayer?)

Einen Moment bitte! (One moment, please.)

Bleiben Sie am Apparat. (Stay on the line.)

Sie haben einen Anruf. (You have a call.)

Sie ist heute nicht im Hause. (She's not in the building today.)

Ihre Durchwahl ist gerade besetzt. (Her extension is presently busy.)

Darf ich eine Nachricht hinterlassen? (May I leave a message?)

When asking to speak with someone, use the correct form of address. Titles are very important to German speakers, especially Austrians. Make an effort to find out how they like to be addressed. Be safe and learn the following forms of address:

Frau = Mrs./Ms.

Herr = Mr.

Dr./Doktor) = Dr./Doctor (Used with all doctors, not just with medical doctors.)

Fräulein = Miss (Used only with children or, in very rare cases, with older women who have never married. It is also used with female service personnel—a sort of feminine "garçon."

REAL CONVERSATIONS

No doubt you're looking forward to your first conversation with real-life German speakers. Maybe you've already overheard some conversations in movies or in public. What characterizes conversation versus written language? Well...umm...let's see here; if you were to write down, like, what most people, umm, say, it would be, well, less than concise and, yeah, rather wordy, right? When Americans converse, they use a lot of fill words to let their brains catch up with their tongues. Germans are no different. You can employ the same trick. Here are the most common German "fill" words:

dann = then

na ja = well

wohl = really

jawohl = indeed

nicht wahr? = isn't that so?

wissen Sie = you know

You can imagine how useful these can be in bridging your thoughts and making you sound like a native:

Na ja, dann gehen wir morgen. (Well, then we go tomorrow.)

Es ist ein warmer Tag, nicht wahr? (It's a warm day, isn't it?)

Es ist wohl warm! (It is really warm!)

Es ist ja Juli, wissen Sie. (It is July, you know.)

Jawohl! (Indeed!)

Try to include these little "fill" words to spice up your spoken German. Don't overdo it, however; they are best used in moderation and should not become a crutch.

PLAYING ROLES

Write a conversation between you and your ideal German-speaking informant. That person could be dead or alive, famous or a relative or an imaginary friend. Query your correspondent and make up the responses he or she might supply you. Be creative, stretch yourself, and have fun. Take a look at the following sample for inspiration:

Dr. Freud	Güten Tag! Mein Name ist Freud. Doktor Sigmund Freud. Willkommen in meiner Praxis! (My name is Freud. Dr. Sigmund Freud. Welcome to my office.)
	Wie geht es Ihnen? (How are you?)
Patient	*Mir geht es nicht so gut, Doktor Freud.* (I'm not doing so well, Dr. Freud.)
Dr. Freud	*Warum?* (Why?)
Patient	*Ich weiß es nicht.* (I don't know.)
Dr. Freud	*Das ist Ihr Problem!* (That is your problem!)

Exercise 1

Next, complete the following incomplete conversation:

Dr. Freud   Guten _____! Mein _____ ist
                  Freud. Dr. Sigmund Freud. _____
                  geht es Ihnen?

QUICK 🔋 PAINLESS

When you don't hear or understand what some-one says, just say *Wie bitte?* (How was that, please?) They will repeat themselves.

Calling someone *mein Freund,* as opposed to *ein Freund,* is rather intimate. Remember: A German friend is a friend for life.

Patient _____ geht es gut. Und Ihnen?

Dr. Freud   Mir geht es _____.

Exercise 2: How Are You Feeling Today?

Use this list to reflect your mood into a German language response:

☺ ☺ Mir geht es sehr gut.

☺ Mir geht es gut.

☹ Mir geht es so-so.

☹ Mir geht es nicht so gut.

☹ ☹ Mir geht es sehr schlecht.

Next, imagine that you meet Dr. Freud and that he wants to get to know you. Respond to his questions with a complete sentence.

Wie ist Ihr Name?

_____

Guten Tag! Wie geht es Ihnen?

_____

Now It's Your Turn

Now that you've been analyzed by Sigmund Freud, it's your turn to make up a conversation with a famous German. Have fun with it! Who do you want to talk to today?

_____

_____

_____

_____

There Are No Problems, Only Solutions

Finding your way out of problems requires you to stretch your vocabulary and get creative. When the going gets tough, the tough get going, right? I'll show you how to manage everyday problems, real emergencies, and business scenarios. And just as an ounce of prevention is worth a pound of cure, I'll teach you some tricks to avoid problems. Then you'll have some fun exploring the workings of the railroad and putting together an itinerary that won't take *nein* for an answer.

EVERYDAY QUESTIONS

You spend most of your days traveling figuring out where to go and how to pay for it when you get there. The rest of the time you have to deal with questions and problems that modify your original plan. Knowing which questions to ask can make getting your answers a snap.

QUICK ⚑ PAINLESS

Want to know why the bus stopped, why the store isn't open, or why there's no hot water? Just ask *Was ist das Problem?* It's easy to remember because it is so similar to the English: "What is the problem?"

Interruptions, Disturbances, and Surprises

You know and I know that even a traveler's best-made plans can fall flat in the face of everyday occurrences such as holidays, strikes, construction, or even a shopkeeper's lunch break. Don't take "no" for an answer, find out "why not." The answer may not really be "no," but just "come back in an hour."

Bummers and Bloopers

Here's all the vocabulary you'll need to figure out why you can't do what you want to do:

ausverkauft = sold out

außer Betrieb = out of order

der Feiertag = holiday

geschlossen = closed (store)

gesperrt = closed (road)

kaputt sein = to be broken

krank sein = to be sick

im Umbau sein = to be under construction/ renovation

die Mittagspause = lunch break

der Streik = strike

umgezogen sein = to have moved

die Verspätung = delay (transportation)

vorbei sein = to be over

Exercise 1

Translate the following sentences (and see how bad news can actually have a happy ending):

Das Museum ist im Umbau. Die Austellung ist aber offen.

_____

Der Zug hat eine Verspätung. Er fährt um 20:20.

_____

Wir haben jetzt Mittagspause. Kommen Sie wieder um 14:00.

_____

Die Karten sind ausverkauft, aber wir haben noch eine fur Sie.

_____

Das kleine Auto ist kaputt. Nehmen Sie das große Auto.

_____

Let's hope that all the dark clouds you encounter on your journey have silver linings like these!

Write It Once, Use It Twice

There are a number of ways to keep from having to ask everyday questions more often than you need to. One way is to be sure you get double use out of your written documents in German. For example, if you are sending a written confirmation of your hotel reservation in German, save a copy to take with you when you check in. This way, you don't have to explain the details again.

Notice the spelling of *kaputt*. It is spelled with two *T*'s in German. This is one of the few examples in which a word that was borrowed from German is misspelled in English. Oops!

To keep all your travel papers in one place, create a binder with your itinerary, reservation confirmations, maps, and other travel documentation. You'll be able to flip through it during your trip and find what you need when you need it. Add postcards, brochures, and souvenirs as you travel, and your scrapbook will be finished by the time you get home.

You should make an extra copy of your itinerary for a relative or the house sitter in case they need to get in touch with you.

And with that, you will have at least three good uses for the same information! Having the details of your trip written down will also prevent your heart from getting stuck in your throat when you march up to the counter!

Counter Talk

Your trip will boil itself down to information provided on a few pieces of paper. These are:

die Bestätigung = confirmation

die Bestellung = order

buchen = to book

die Kopie = copy

der Reiseweg = itinerary

die Reservierung = reservation

Exercise 2

Translate these phrases into German for some practice telling people on the other side of the counter that you are in charge!

Here is my confirmation.

_____

Here is the copy of the order.

_____

Do you have my itinerary?

_____

Where is the copy?

_____

You have the copy of the confirmation.

_____

REAL PROBLEMS

So far, the problems I've told you how to fix are pretty minor. What do you do when you have real problems? Get help! It's always a good idea to know how to summon the troops when you need them.

Getting Help

When you need help, you need it. So work with the verb *brauchen* (to need). Thankfully, it is regular.

Brauchen (to need)	Singular	Plural
First person	ich brauche	wir brauchen
Second person (informal)	du brauchst	ihr braucht
Second person (formal)	Sie brauchen	
Third person	er, sie, es braucht	sie brauchen

QUICK  PAINLESS

When you enter your destination, march up to the counter and say, *Ich habe eine Reservierung.* It's easy to remember because it sounds like "I have a reservation." And, it puts the ball in the clerk's court. Let him ask the next question!

You can combine *brauchen* with the following emergency services to summon almost any help you might need:

die Apotheke = pharmacy

der Arzt = doctor

die Feuerwehr = fire department

das Krankenhaus = hospital

der Krankenwagen = ambulance

die Polizei = police

Exercise 3

Translate the following emergency requests. Hopefully, you will never need to use them!

We need the police.

_____

She needs an ambulance.

_____

He needs a pharmacy.

_____

They need a doctor.

_____

We need a hospital.

_____

Better Safe Than Sorry

You can prevent a lot of the hassles of losing important documents or cash if you just take measures to carry them carefully. Invest in a money belt and secure your loot. You can also put important items in the hotel safe for secure storage.

Another good idea is to make two copies of your passport. Leave one at home with your itinerary and carry one with you. If your original passport is lost or stolen, you can replace it easily. Who wants to spend his or her vacation at the consulate?

BUSINESS MATTERS

If you are in business, you are used to solving problems. You just need to transfer those skills into learning German. How bad could a business question be in Germany? Working in Germany isn't so bad. They do get six weeks of paid vacation, after all. Maybe you can arrange a transfer?

Trade Show Lingo

Germany is famous for its world-class trade shows; from technology to forestry there is a show for almost every industry. Trade shows attract companies from around the world to trade show facilities from Hamburg to Munich. As anyone who has been to a monster trade show knows, finding your way around and getting to the top events can be a challenge. You'll make it easier on yourself if you go into it knowing the vocabulary:

IF YOU'RE SO
INCLINED

Take a look at all the trade shows in Germany. Maybe one of them will be going on while you are in Europe, and your boss will pay for part of your trip. Wouldn't that be nice? For more information, go online and check out http://www.messe.de/

You can often check all the details of your itinerary by going on the Internet to see the current open times and impending changes. Things can still change, but at least you will be as up-to-date as possible with your plans. It can save a lot of trouble later.

die Auskunft = information booth

der Austeller = exhibitor

der Austellungsprogramm = show program

der Besucher = visitor

die Firma = company

die Führung = tour

die Messe = trade show

das Messegelände = trade show facility

die Halle = hall

das Muster = sample, prototype

der Stand = booth

die Tagung = meeting

der Termin = appointment

der Vortrag = lecture

die Werbung = advertisement

Here's a sample conversation for you to read aloud. Notice the problem-solving skills the visitor applies in this dialogue.

Besucher	*Entschuldigung! Wo ist der Stand von der Firma Infostix?*
(Visitor)	(Excuse me! Where is the booth for the Infostix company?)
Auskunft	*Halle C, Stand 393. Sehen Sie die Halle C hier in dem Ausstellungsprogramm? Ja, dort ist es.*

(Information)	(Hall C, booth 393. Do you see Hall C here in the show program? That's where it is.)
Besucher	*Ja, aber das Messegelände ist sehr groß. Wie trage ich alles bis Halle C?*
(Visitor)	Yes, but the trade show facility is very large. How can I carry all this to Hall C?)
Auskunft	*Ein Bus macht eine kleine Führung der Messe. Fahren Sie doch mit!*
(Information)	(A bus makes a small tour of the trade show. Just go along!)
Besucher	*Diese Messe ist sehr besucherfreundlich.*
(Visitor)	(This trade show is very visitor-friendly.)
Auskunft	*Sie sind Besucher? Dann geht es nicht. Nur Aussteller können den Bus nehmen.*
(Information)	(You're a visitor? Then that won't work. Only exhibitors can take the bus.)
Besucher	*Besucher? Ich bin kein Besucher!*
(Visitor)	(Visitor? I am not a visitor!)

WORKING WITH THE RAILROAD

Public transportation in Germany, Austria, Luxembourg, and Switzerland is easy, fast, and efficient—if you can decipher the schedules, that is.

A COMPLETE WASTE OF TIME

The worst things you can do when your travels don't go as planned are to:

1. Let it get you down. The difference between a good day and a bad day is your attitude. *Lächeln!* (Smile!)

2. Forget your creative question-asking skills. Ask *warum?* (Why?)

3. Neglect to ask about your options. *Gibt es andere Möglichkeiten? (possibilities?)*

All of these German-speaking countries have well-developed national rail systems with seamless or nearly seamless connections to regional and local bus and light rail systems, public ferry systems, and other forms of travel (for example, funicular railways, cable lifts, and so on). In fact, rail travel is so civilized and comfortable in these countries that you'll wonder why Americans ever got so crazy about the automobile in the first place. The only challenges are reading the schedules and choosing from the many routes and itineraries to get from point Aachen to point Bern.

One option is to buy a universal rail pass. (The "Eurail" pass is a good choice for Americans, but it must be purchased on this side of the Atlantic.) Another approach is to mix and match from among the many kinds of ticketing options. This also makes an interesting problem-solving activity that will improve your German. You'll want to ask about special offers, such as off-peak travel, group or family discounts, and reduced fares for seniors and children.

You can get German rail schedules from a good travel agency, or view them online at http://www.bahn.de/. With schedule in hand, plan a trip from a smaller city or town (Ingolstadt or Aachen, perhaps) to a larger city (Hannover or Berlin, for example). You will find many types of *Züge* (trains) from which to choose. Older, slower *D-Züge* offer the opportunity for more leisurely sightseeing, while *IC-Züge* (Inter-City trains) travel the same route but much faster and at different times. For the ultimate in speed and comfort, Germany's high-speed

QUICK 🐷 PAINLESS

One phrase you'll be able to use again and again in business situations is, *Geschäft ist Geschäft* (business is business). Not only is it catchy, it makes you sound like you know what you're talking about!

Inter-City-Express (*ICE*) is the way to go. Of course, the itinerary you select may require travel on all three trains, as well as on the local *S-Bahn* (regional rail) and urban *U-Bahn* (subway).

When planning your itinerary, be sure to calculate the cost of both *ein einfaches* (a one-way ticket) and *eine Rückfahrkarte* (a round-trip ticket). Some faster trains require *einen Zuschlag* (additional fee), and, of course, first and second class passengers pay different fares. Finally, trains at peak hours have more convenient—and hence more expensive—arrival (*Ankunft*) and departure (*Abfahrt*) times

They say the trains in Germany always run on time. For the most part this is true. Given the thoroughness and complexity of German rail tables, however, it's a wonder anyone has time to ride the trains. If you can solve the problems in this activity, you might be more German than you think.

Now for Something Completely Different: Celebrating in German

Everyone likes to celebrate, and German-speaking people are world champions at partying—from the famous Oktoberfest to Christmas celebrations. You will certainly enjoy fun and excitement if you are lucky enough to be present at a German celebration.

THE PARTY SCENE

If you are less than well connected in the art, political, or business world, you may not have pressing party engagements in Berlin, Hamburg, and Munich next year. What are you to do? Don't be a wallflower and stay in your hotel and mope. Find some happening events near you. Check out the paper and local events calendars for events that sound promising. Cultural institutes, universities, galleries, museums and so forth often advertise highlights. Many are free, and some

When searching for celebrations and parties:

1. Don't expect there to be as many celebrations in the winter as in the summer. There are a few for Christmas and New Year's, but that's about it.

2. Don't forget to look for celebrations around church holidays. Parades and processions often mark traditional holy days.

3. Don't skip over your professional association or service club. They might have a branch in Europe that holds regular meetings.

include champagne and appetizers. Dress up and you'll be welcome. Here are some to look for:

der Empfang = reception

die Eröffnung = opening

die Erstaufführung = premiere

das Jubiläum = anniversary celebration

die Vernissage = art opening

Other things to look for are parties in their own right. There are numerous examples of them in Germany; just look at all the words that mean "party:

das Fest = party

die Party = party

die Fete = party

das Feier = party

When one of these words is part of a compound noun, it is time to let the good times roll! *Winterfest*, *Weinfest*, *Folksfest*, and *Oktoberfest* are all opportunities to celebrate. The many local celebrations are too numerous to list. There are celebrations throughout the year, many of which center around Christian holidays. Christmas in Germany is a remarkable affair, with *Weihnachtsmärkte* (Christmas craft markets) set up in public squares. You can enjoy concerts, traditional baked specialties, such as *Lebkuchen* (a soft gingerbread-like cookie), and real candles on the *Tannenbaum*. You are certain to bump into some celebrations while you are in Germany, even if you don't search them out.

GERMAN KUSTOMS

Food and drink are the traditional German focus at a party. If the party is held at a private home, you may want to bring a small gift for the hosts. At public events expect bountiful buffets brimming with cold cuts, cheeses, and delicious open-faced sandwiches. In the north, you can expect fish, while in the south expect an array of sausages. Follow the lead of the other guests and help yourself; then, single out some interesting folks for conversation.

Party Small Talk

You can get the small talk going with a simple compliment about the event. You don't even have to use a complete sentence. Try one of the following:

Tolles Essen! (Fantastic food!)

Wunderbare Musik! (Wonderful music!)

Nette Leute! (Nice people!)

Schöne Umgebung! (Beautiful surroundings!)

Be the Toast of the Party

An easy way to be part of the party is to propose a toast. You can keep it simple or add your favorite twist. When lifting your glass, highlight the moment with a German classic:

Prost! (Cheers!)

Zum Wohl! (To your health!)

Schau mir in die Augen kleines! (Here's looking at you, kid!)

IF YOU'RE SO
INCLINED

Send a German-speaking friend or relative a birthday card in German. Just write, *Alles Gute zum Geburtstag!* (Best wishes on your Birthday!) Maybe she'll invite you to a party where you can work on your German skills.

BEER AND WINE

Germany is probably most famous for its beer. There are so many kinds of beer that you could practically try one each day of your visit. Because the Germans have such a strong presence in the brewing world, even English-speaking beer connoisseurs will be familiar with these German terms:

ein alkoholfreies Bier = non-alcoholic beer

ein Alt = top-fermented, dark beer

ein Bock = bock

ein Dunkles = dark beer

ein Helles = light-colored beer

ein Lager = lager

ein Malzbier = malt beer

das Pils = pilsner

das Weizenbier = wheat beer

So how do you want it? Whether you lift your stein in the *Hofbräuhaus* or in a *Biergarten* you'll have a lot of choices: large or small, draft or bottle? To order, use your old friend, the irregular verb *mögen*, as follows:

Ich möchte ein großes Bier vom Faß bitte. (I'd like a large draft beer.)

Impress the bartender with these terms:

die Flasche = bottle

ein großes Bier = a large beer

ein kleines Bier = a small beer

YOU'LL THANK YOURSELF LATER

When you are invited to a party, it is customary to bring flowers or a bottle of wine. Don't bring chrysanthemums, however; they are considered funeral flowers.

vom Faß = draft

eine Maß = a southern German/Austrian liter-sized beer in a stein

Wein Muß Sein

German wines have long gotten short "shrift" abroad. (Hey, that's a Yiddish word from the German word *die Schrift* [writing].) The tide is turning, however; wine tasters around the world now appreciate the fine white and, yes, red wines of Germany, Austria, and Switzerland. Most of the wineries in these countries are small and still owned by independent families, which means the best wines are seldom available for export. Therefore, you should make a point of sampling the best of the local wines during your trip.

The most famous wine-growing regions are along Germany's Mosel, Rhine, and Neckar Rivers. The vines climb terraced hills so steep that they must be tended and harvested by hand. Some of the varieties to sample include:

Weißweine (White Wines)

Gewürztraminer

Müller-Thurgau

Riesling

Rotweine (Red Wines)

Portugieser

Spätburgunder

Trollinger

IF YOU'RE SO INCLINED

Talk to your local wine merchant about German, Swiss, or Austrian wines. Buy a few bottles and have a wine-tasting party. You can also find cheeses from German-speaking countries and educate yourself on regional specialties while you enjoy an evening of gourmet delights.

Food-purity laws have a long tradition in Germany. Beer is subject to the *Reinheitsgebot* (Purity Law). Drafted in 1516, it states that the only ingredients that can be used in beer are hops, barley, yeast, and water.

You can find good German wine by stopping into a fine restaurant or *Weinstube* (wine pub), or by ambling along the famous *Weinstraßen* (wine roads). You can visit *ein Weingut* (wine estate) for *eine Probe* (wine tasting), or buy a few bottles at *ein Flaschenverkauf* (English translation). The following terms will help you decide on a variety:

fruchtig = fruity

harmonisch = well-balanced

herb = austere

die Säure = acidity

Sortencharakter = with characteristics of the vine variety

trocken = dry

Ways to Say You're Drunk

Among the first things many of my college students asked me about German was how to order beer. The next was how to say "I'm drunk!" Many Americans are not accustomed to Germany's strong beer and overdo their sampling. Remember two things: Yes, you can get a hangover even though you are on vacation, and never drink and drive in Europe. Don't drink and drive anywhere, but especially not in Europe; the rules are even stricter than in the United States.

The Beer Index

Ich bin beschwipst. (I am tipsy.)

Ich bin blau. (I am blue.)

Zu tief in den Glas schauen. (To look too deep into the glass.)

Ich bin besoffen. (I am drunk.)

But all good things must come to an end, and hopefully you take good memories with you. Next, I'll show you how to cope with too much of a good thing.

The Morning After

Hopefully, you won't suffer any ailments, but the minor consequences of overeating and overdrinking are common travel ailments. You can find all the remedies you need at the *Apotheke* (pharmacy). Simply describe your condition to the *Apotheker* (pharmacist), as follows:

Leichte Erkrankungen (Ailments)

Ich habe Kopfschmerzen. (I have a headache.)

Ich habe Magenschmerzen. (I have a stomachache.)

Ich habe Verdauungsprobleme. (I have digestion problems.)

Ich habe Durchfall. (I have diarrhea.)

Heilmittel (Remedies)

Travel medications you may need include:

das Abführmittel = laxative

das Antazidum = antacid

das Aspirin = aspirin

das Schlafmittel = sleeping aid

QUICK  PAINLESS

You can spot pharmacies in German-speaking countries by looking for big white signs with a red letter A (for *Apotheke*).

Exercise 2

Now that you have the vocabulary to manage the minor illnesses that may come your way, try translating these scenarios:

I have a headache. I need an aspirin.

_____

I have digestion problems. I need a laxative.

_____

I need a sleeping aid.

_____

I need an antacid.

_____

I have a stomachache. Do you have a remedy?

_____

THE FINALE: EIN DEUTSCHES FEST

Drum roll, please! You are a graduate of *German The Lazy Way*. I have tried to make the process as easy on you as possible. Your last assignment is to throw a party. What's the catch? You must do it German style! You'll find it easier to throw your party if you pick a theme. You may want to schedule it to coincide with the classic German holidays: Oktoberfest or Christmas. It could be Swiss fondue in front of the fireplace, an Alpine hike and picnic, or a *Biergarten* on a warm evening under the trees. Pick a theme that suits your style, and get started.

Once you have a theme, make your guest list. You can have as few as one guest or as many as you can pack into your beer-hall tent! It's up to you. You can celebrate your upcoming trip to Europe or your recent return. Welcome guests from Europe or just invite your well-traveled friends. To make the job easier, consider making it a gourmet potluck. Assign guests different courses and encourage them to search out German recipes from their families or cookbooks. (See Chapter 13 for ideas on where to find German food.) Highlight German beverages, from fine beer and wine to mineral water. Whatever your theme, send out bilingual invitations.

It'll be easy; simply follow this template for a fun, casual invitation:

Achtung! (Attention!)

Am 1. März um 18:00 Uhr, veranstalten wir ein deutsches Fest.

(On March 1 at 6:00 p.m., we are having a German party.)

Es gibt gutes Bier, deutsches Essen und zünftige Musik.

(There will be good beer, German food, and traditional music.)

u.A.w.g.

R.S.V.P.

Feel free to vary the idea and come up with your own theme-based invitation. You may want guests to come in traditional German dress or bring photos from a recent

Congratulations on completing your course in *German The Lazy Way*. You deserve a night out! Throw a simple celebration by making reservations at a local German restaurant or pub. Take a friend and celebrate your accomplishments in German.

trip to Germany. And get ready to dance! You'll be ready to play German music after our exercise in exploring the world of German tunes in Chapter 1.

If you get enough German-speakers together, you can even make German the official language for the evening. You'll be launching yourself into the real world of the German language with style—the lazy way.

More Lazy Stuff

How to Get Someone Else to Do It

You don't have to be a delegate of the United Nations to benefit from an interpreter or translator. Learn how to find a qualified language professional to help you cross the language barrier. To a limited extent, translation programs can help out in a pinch. I'll show you how to make them work for you. In addition, I'll tell you about electronic reference tools that can help you find what you need fast.

HIRING A PRO

Sometimes it is best to leave the job of a foreign language to a pro. But how do you find one? The following tips will help you find a person with the proper language and subject knowledge to get your project across the finish line:

- Use the Internet's searchable databases of translators and interpreters. Two good sites to check out are:

    http://www.rahul.net/lai/ncta/trdb.htm

    http://aquarius.net/

- Check the Yellow Pages under translation/interpretation services

■ Ask your local college or university language departments for referrals

AGENCY OR INDIVIDUAL?

When looking for quality translation, you can go directly to a translator over the Internet and eliminate the middle man of the translation agency. Note, however, that anyone can call himself a translator and perform linguistic acts of violence to your text. Advantages of using an agency include:

■ Team translation with an independent proofreader and editor

■ Professional project management and translator screening

■ The ability to handle larger volumes of work

QUALITY QUALIFICATIONS

Regardless of whether you choose an agency or a lone translator, look for professionals who:

■ Work only in one language pair and into their native language.

■ Have trained and lived extensively with their language. (Look for professional training at a graduate level.)

■ Quote a word rate for translation or a per diem rate for interpretation, and provide a written cost estimate and turnaround.

■ Ask you questions, such as what the purpose of your translation is. If it's for casual information or publication there will be a different target audience for the translation.

Look for a well-trained translator who is a member of a professional organization, such as the American Translator's Association. Be sure to check on a translator's references.

ONLINE TRANSLATION ENGINES

Although online translation programs are not recommended, they can be useful in a pinch.

Some search engines, such as AltaVista, offer links to online translation programs that may help you with a simple translation of an email or Web site. Beware, however, that these programs are useful only to a very limited extent and may translate material inaccurately due to the complexity of human language. In short, always double-check important documents with a human translator. If you must use a translation program, always preface any document translated by machine with a disclaimer stating: "This document was translated by a software program." Also attach an English version of the text so that your reader can refer to it, as necessary.

You can find the AltaVista translator program at:

http://babelfish.altavista.com/cgi-bin/translate?

Here's a sample of the program's translation skills when it comes to translating a simple text from English into German:

Hi Andreas. We'll come visit you in Berlin on March 21.

Hallo Andreas. Wir kommen Besuch Sie in Berlin an März 21.

This translation is understandable nonsense. A proper translation would be:

Hallo Andreas. Wir besuchen Dich am 21. März in Berlin.

And here's what you get when you trust a machine translating German into English:

Liebe Amy,

Wir kommen Dich am 21. März besuchen.

Bis dann!

Andreas

Dear Amy, we comes to the attendance on 21 March. Until then!
Andreas

No comment. With some imagination, however, you can sort of guess at the meaning of the translation.

TRANSLATION SOFTWARE

Programs that promise translation miracles are not recommended, use with caution.

Programs are available for use on your home PC, but the results are usually disappointing.

ELECTRONIC REFERENCE TOOLS

While translation software may not be as useful as hoped, electronic reference works, such as CD-ROM dictionaries or online glossaries, offer a fast way to look up terminology. Remember that anyone can publish on the Web and that all dictionaries are not created equal, particularly those that encourage user input. Two of the more useful online resources are:

- **Meyers German Encyclopedia:** A resource in German available at http://www.iicm.edu/ref.m10

- **Langenscheidt New College German Dictionary:** A bilingual dictionary available at http://www.lhs-lt.de/en/products/t1woerter.htm

To order specialized dictionaries on almost any language you can think of, check out http://www.ibdltd.com.

Getting someone else to do the job has never been so easy!

If You Really Want More, Read These

Half the battle is finding the right books, resources, and supplies. There are a lot of resources for learning more advanced German. Check out these valuable precision German learning tools If you want more good language information. Web resources offer a healthy supply of free stuff in and about German.

MODERN MEDIA

Some of the best resources on German culture are compiled at www.german-way.com. It features information on German, Austrian, and Swiss culture, with a comprehensive list of links to lead you to more information about Germanic topics than you will ever need.

For resources about the German language, I refer you to my Web site, www.globalaccent.com for related Web links and expanded information.

PRINTED RESOURCES

The following annotated list of books will get you started toward building your library of books on things German.

Culture

- *The German Way* (by Hyde Flippo): A summary of life and culture in Austria, Germany and Switzerland.

- *The Xenophobe's Guide to the Germans* (by S. Zeidenitz and B. Barkow): A less serious look at Germans.

Dictionaries

- *Cassell's German-English, English-German Dictionary* (by Harold T. Betteridge): One of the best one-volume dictionaries.

- *Langenscheidt Compact German Dictionary* (by Langenscheidt Publishers): A solid dictionary for serious students of German.

- *Langenscheidt New College German-English, English-German Dictionary* (by Langenscheidt Publishers): A classic, well-researched dictionary.

Grammar Books

- *English Grammar for Students of German* (by Cecile Zorach): Detailed explanations of how English works that will make learning German grammar easier. Very highly recommended.

- *Schaum's Outline of German Grammar* (by Elke Gschossmann-Hendershot, Lois M. Feuerle): A classic grammar summary.

- *1001 Pitfalls in German* (by Henry Strutz): A good outline of mistakes you should avoid.

- *2001 German and English Idioms* (by Henry Strutz): Idioms are tricky because they don't translate literally. Check out this extensive list.

- *501 German Verbs* (by Henry Strutz): Regular or irregular, they are in here.

Activities

- *Easy German Word Games & Puzzles* (by Susanne Ehrlich): Make learning German fun for yourself or your students.

- *German for the Business Traveler* (by Henry Strutz): More details for the business person.

- *German for Children* (by Catherine Bruzzone): Play and sing German for kids.

- *Let's Learn German Coloring Book* (by Anne-Francoise Hazzan): Children love to play with both language and crayons at the same time.

Phrase Books

- *Scheisse! The Real German You Were Never Taught in School* (by Getrude Besserwisser): Phrases you should use with caution.

- *Wicked German* (by Howard Tomb): This phrase book won't take *verboten* for an answer.

- *Jiffy Phrasebook German* (by Langenscheidt Publishers): An inexpensive but useful phrase book.

If You Don't Know What It Means, Look Here

Sure, you knew that. *Natürlich!* But here's a quick refresher course in case you don't immediately remember the difference between a direct object and an indirect object.

Accusative The case used for direct objects and the objects of some prepositions.

Adjective A descriptive word that modifies a noun or pronoun. German adjectives are modified to reflect the case of the noun.

Adverb A descriptive word that modifies a verb. Thankfully, German adverbs are lazy and never change their form.

Article A word placed before a noun that indicates whether the noun refers to a specific item (definite article: *the*) or an unspecified item (indefinite article: *a*).

Case The grammatical function of a noun or pronoun in a sentence. The form of the word itself and the words that accompany it indicate the case. There are four cases in German: nominative, genitive, dative, and accusative. And yes, there are enough of them to fill a monster-sized case.

Cognate   Related words, or "kissing cousins," from the same family of languages. For example: *der Finger* (finger).

Conjugation   A complete paradigm showing a verb in each number, person, voice, mood, and tense.

Conjunction   A word, such as "and" or "but," that links phrases or clauses.

Dative   Used for indirect objects, the objects of some prepositions, and the objects of some verbs.

Declension   A complete paradigm showing an adjective or noun in all of its cases.

Definite article   A word placed before a noun to indicate a specific item. For example: *der Apfel*, *die Äpfel* (the apple, the apples).

Direct object   A noun that is directly affected by the action expressed by the verb. For example: He ate *the apple*.

Eszett   The name for the German double *s* or *ß*. It looks like a beta but is equivalent to *ss*.

Feminine   The feminine grammatical gender is indicated by the feminine article *die*.

Future tense   The conjugation of a verb that indicates the action will occur at a future time.

Gender   A grammatical category that determines how a noun and the adjectives used with it will be declined to indicate the four different cases. German has three genders: masculine (indicated in the nominative case by the article *der*), feminine (*die*), and neuter (*das*). "Gender" has nothing to do with the biological sense of the word.

Genitive   The case used to show possession and the objects of some prepositions.

Idiom   A fixed expression that does not translate literally. For example: "It's raining cats and dogs."

Indefinite article   A word placed before a noun to indicate an unspecified item. For example" *ein Apfel* (an apple). There is no plural of the indefinite article.

Indirect object   A noun or pronoun that is the recipient of the action. For example: "She gave the apple to *him*."

Infinitive   The unconjugated form of a verb. For example: *sein* (to be).

Masculine   The masculine grammatical gender is indicated by the masculine article *der*.

Modal verb   This auxiliary verb reflects the attitude, or mode (thus, *modal*), of the speaker about the main verb in the sentence. For example: "can," "should," and "may."

Mood   The form of a verb used to indicate the speaker's attitude toward the factuality or likelihood of the action or condition expressed. The *indicative mood* is used for statements of fact; the *subjunctive mood* is used to indicate doubt or possibility; and the *imperative mood* is used to issue commands.

Neuter   The neuter grammatical gender is indicated by the neuter article *das*.

Nominative   The case used for the subject of the sentence or a predicate noun.

Noun   A person, place, or thing. German nouns are masculine, feminine, or neuter in gender.

Number   The grammatical term for the categories of singular and plural. Number can refer to nouns (*der Apfel*, *die Äpfel*, the apple/the apples) or verbs (*ich bin/wir sind*, I am/we are).

Past tense   The conjugation of a verb that indicates an action occurred at an earlier time.

Person   First, second, and third person are the three groups of pronoun forms. They allow the speaker to distinguish between the speaker (first person: *I*, *we*), the individual addressed (second person: *you*, *you all*), and the individual or thing spoken about (third person: *he*, *she*, *it*, or *they*).

Plural   The number of a noun or verb used to show there is more than one.

Predicate noun   A noun that refers back to the subject of the sentence. For example: "This is *a great book*." Predicate nouns are expressed in the nominative case in German, as are the subjects to which they point.

Present tense   The conjugation of a verb that indicates the action is occurring at the present time.

Pronoun   A word used in the place of one or more nouns, Hans and Franz came. <u>They</u> came.

Singular   The number of a noun or verb used to show there is just one.

Subject   The noun or pronoun that performs the action in a sentence.

Tense   An important function of the verb is to indicate the time of an action. The *tense* refers to the way the verb is conjugated to express this meaning. *Tense* is also something you should never be when learning German the lazy way.

Umlaut   Those two cute dots you see over some vowels in German. For example: ö, ü, and ä. It is equivalent to adding an *e* to the vowel and shifting the sound forward in your mouth.

Verb   A word that expresses existence or action in a sentence.

It's Time for Your Reward: Answer Key

CHAPTER TWO

Exercise 1

A friend's telephone number: fünf zwei drei sieben acht acht zwei (for example)

Your address: vier null eins Mill Street (for example)

Your birth date: zwölf fünf achtundsechzig (Remember that the day comes before the month in German-style calendaring.)

Your high school graduation year: neunzehnhunderteinundsiebzig (for example)

Exercise 2

Dezember

Montag	7	14	21	28
Dienstag	1	8	15	22	29
Mittwoch	2	9	16	23	30
Donnerstag	3	10	17	24 Heiligabend	31 Silvester
Freitag	4	11	18	25 Weihnachten	
Samstag	5	12	19	26	
Sonntag	6 Nikolaustag	13	20	27	

CHAPTER FIVE

Tag (day)

Nagel (nail)

Tee (tea)

Wolf (wolf)

fangen (to catch)

gehen (to go)

joggen (to jog)

etc.

CHAPTER SIX

Exercise 1

I have an old houseboat. It is summer. It is a hot night. Father and uncle bring wine and beer. My bed is soft. We sleep. The door is open. A thief comes. The thief wants my silver. The moon shines. He sees silver. He is dumb. He has my fish!

Exercise 2

Tief_es_ Wasser (deep water)

Kalt_es_ Fleisch (cold meat; "flesh" is the cognate for "Fleisch")

Gut_en_ Tag! (Good day!)

Apfelkuchen (apple cake)

Exercise 3

I am a hacker. I fax you a computer magazine. Or do you want it from the Internet? The cover is really clever. Do you see the list with tips and tricks? And my photo? I am the big boss here. A super hit. Totally cool. My job is okay, man.

Exercise 4

There once was a (*adjective*: nice) (*adjective*: young) man who was trying to learn German so that he could take a trip to (*proper noun*: Europe) with his (*noun*: family). He was very busy at the law (*noun*: firm) where he was trying to (*verb*: make) (*noun*: partner). His (*noun*: boss) was a really wonderful (*noun*: man) but had no idea how much (*noun*: energy) and time it takes to raise (*noun*: children). His boss insisted that he come in on (*plural noun*: weekends) and late at night to (*verb*: write) reports on important cases.

Our blossoming lawyer was a (*noun*: specialist) in patent law. His clients were (*adjective*: interesting) multinational corporations. In fact, he often (*verb*: spoke) with (*plural noun*: colleagues) in Zurich, Munich, and Vienna on the (*noun*: telephone). Their English was so good that it really (*verb*: motivated) him to want to learn more German.

But where could he (*verb*: find) the time? A (*noun*: friend) told him that if he could find excuses he could find time to (*verb*: learn). With a (*season*: summer) vacation trip planned to Germany and Austria, he had great motivation to (*verb*: master) at least the basics. Once he got (*verb*: started), he was shocked to see how much he already knew. Why had they kept this a secret from him in (*noun*: school)?

CHAPTER SEVEN
Exercise 1

Ich habe den Tisch.

Ich habe das Bild.

Ich habe den Stift.

Ich habe die Postkarte.

Ich habe die Uhr.

Ich habe die Lampen.

Exercise 2

Ich habe die Lampe.

Ich habe die Heizung.

Ich habe den Tisch.

Ich habe das Bild.

Ich habe die Uhr.

Ich habe das Buch.

Exercise 3

Ich habe einen Tisch.

Ich habe ein Bild.

Ich habe einen Stift.

Ich habe eine Postkarte.

Ich habe eine Uhr.

Exercise 4

Ich habe eine Lampe.

Ich habe einen Tisch.

Ich habe eine Tür.

Ich habe eine Uhr.

Ich habe ein Buch.

Ich habe einen Stift.

Exercise 5

Wir haben kein Zimmer.

Sie haben keinen Stift.

Das Zimmer hat kein Fenster.

Ich habe keine Zimmer.

CHAPTER EIGHT

Exercise 1

I see only water.

It is already Monday.

Maybe it is the house.

He is always fast.

Now it is summer.

Exercise 2

(Diese) Tage sind schön.

Ich gebe dem Kind (diesen) Apfel.

Ich gebe (diesem) Mann das Brot.

(Dieses) Haus ist groß.

Die Tür (dieses) Autos ist kaputt.

Exercise 3

Sie ist *meine* Mutter. Sie ist die Tochter *meines* Opas. Sie ist auch die Schwester *meiner* Tante. In *meiner* Familie gibt es keine Kinder.

Exercise 4

Der *große* Mann spielt Basketball.

Dieses *gute* Buch ist auch billig.

Manche *schnellen* Autos sind sehr teuer.

Ich habe das *kleine* Mädchen.

Wir sind die *besten* Studenten.

Exercise 5

Ich habe ein *altes* Kleid.

Ein *junger* Mann ist hier.

Meine *roten* Rosen sind sehr schön.

Ich habe keine *kleine* Rose.

Deine *helle* Jacke ist sehr chic.

CHAPTER NINE

Exercise 1

Emilie *möchte* eine Lampe. Die zwei Kinder *möchten* Äpfel. Mein
Vater und ich *möchten* Apfelkuchen und Kaffee. Was *möchtest* du?

Exercise 2

Ich kann schlaften.

Wir können gehen.

Können wir es kaufen?

Dürfen wir kommert?

Sie will es bringen.

Exercise 3

1998 *war* ich in Deutschland. München und Berlin *waren* sehr schön.
Es *war* Sommer. Die Tage *waren* sehr lange. Wo *warst* du im Sommer
1998? *War* es auch schön?

Exercise 4

Ich *hatte* ein Haus in Berlin.

Wir *hatten* auch einen Garten.

Er *hatte* einen Apfelbaum.

Exercise 5

I will love it.

We will see Berlin.

You will be a good friend.

Will Karin and Peter come?

The baby will be good.

CHAPTER TEN

Exercise 1

We (*subject*) took (*verb*) a trip (*direct object*) to Europe (*prepositional
object*) last summer (*complement*).

Our plane (*subject*) landed (*verb*) in Frankfurt (*prepositional object*).
The trip (*subject*) was (*verb*) much too short (*complement*). I (*subject*)
loved (*verb*) Germany (*direct object*). I (*subject*) bought (*verb*) a cuckoo clock (*direct object*) for my office (*prepositional object*). I (*subject*)
mailed (*verb*) my friends (*indirect object*) postcards (*direct object*). I
(*subject*) want (*verb*) to go back! Have (*verb*) you (*subject*) been to
Germany (*prepositional object*)?

Exercise 2

Ist das mein Auto?

Bist Du Berliner?

Sind Sie Herr Frank?

Ist das meine Telefonnummer?

CHAPTER TWELVE

Exercise 1

Wir reisen von Hamburg nach Berlin.

Ich gehen von der Schweiz nach Österreich.

Er reist von Deutschland in die Schweiz.

Sie reist von Köln nach Frankfurt.

Exercise 2

Österreich (Austria), Bayern (Bavaria), Braunschweig (Brunswick), Donau (Danube), Köln (Cologne), München (Munich), Rhein (Rhine), Schweiz (Switzerland), Westfalen (Westphalia), Wien (Vienna), Zürich (Zurich)

CHAPTER THIRTEEN

Exercise 1

Entschuldigung, wo ist ein warmes Cafe?

Entschuldigung, wo ist ein billiges Lokal?

Entschuldigung, wo ist das nächste Restaurant?

Entschuldigung, wo ist der Ratskeller?

Entschuldigung, wo ist das Hofbräuhaus?

Exercise 2

Eine Serviette, bitte.

Eine Gabel, bitte.

Ein Löffel, bitte.

Eine Speisekarte, bitte.

Ein Messer, bitte.

Exercise 3

Brot, bitte.

Wasser, bitte.

Salz, bitte.

Bier, bitte.

Milch, bitte.

CHAPTER FOURTEEN

Exercise 1

Das paßt Ihnen.

Gefällt das Ihnen?

Es gefällt uns. Or: Uns gefällt es.

Das steht ihr.

Das paßt ihm.

Exercise 2

Ich schaue mich um.

Du ziehst dich an. or Sie ziehen sich an.

Er bedient sich.

Wir waschen uns.

Sie zieht sich an.

Exercise 3

Ich möchte eine Kuckucksuhr.

Ich möchte eine Postkarte.

Ich möchte einen Bierkrug.

Ich möchte ein Taschenmesser.

Exercise 4

Der Schal ist aus Seide.

Der Hut ist aus Wolle.

Die Jacke ist aus Leder.

Die Hose ist aus Baumwolle.

Das Kleid ist aus Viskose.

Exercise 5

Ich kaufe die Jacke. Ich trage *sie*.

Wir kaufen die Schuhe. Wir tragen *sie*.

Sie kauft das Hemd. Sie trägt *es*.

Er kauft den Schal. Er trägt *ihn*.

Du kaufst den Hut. Du trägst *ihn*.

CHAPTER FIFTEEN

Exercise 1

For example:

Ich sehe eine Burg. Ich sehe auch einen See und eine Insel. Die Burg hat einen Turm.

Exercise 2

We eat in the cafe.

The lake with the island is very beautiful.

After the concert, we are going to Stuttgart.

It is two kilometers from the hotel.

I have been in Austria since that evening.

Exercise 3

der Berg ohne die Burg

durch den Fluß

um den Wald

für das Museum

bis das Konzert

Exercise 4

Ich gehe in die Kirche.

Ich bin in der Kirche.

Wir sind unter der Brücke.

Wir gehen unter die Brücke.

Exercise 5

Das Wetter im Winter ist kalt. Es ist auch nicht sonnig.

Das Wetter im Sommer ist heiß. Es ist sonnig und schön.

CHAPTER SIXTEEN

Dr. Freud	Guten *Tag*! Mein *Name* ist Freud. Dr. Sigmund Freud. *Wie* geht es Ihnen?
Patient	*Mir* geht es gut. Und Ihnen?
Dr. Freud	Mir geht es *gut*.

CHAPTER SEVENTEEN

Exercise 1

The museum is under construction. The exhibit is open, however.

The train has a delay. It is going at 20:20.

We have lunch break now. Come again at 14:00.

The tickets are sold out, but we have one more for you.

The small car is kaput. Take the big car.

Exercise 2

Hier ist meine Bestätigung.

Hier ist die Kopie der Bestellung.

Haben Sie meinen Reiseplan?

Wo ist die Kopie?

Sie haben eine Kopie der Bestätigung.

Exercise 3

Wir brauchen die Polizei.

Sie braucht einen Krankenwagen.

Er braucht eine Apotheke.

Sie brauchen einen Arzt.

Wir brauchen ein Krankenhaus.

CHAPTER EIGHTEEN

Exercise 1

Ich habe Kopfschmerzen. Ich brauche Aspirin.

Ich habe Verdauungsschwierigkeiten. Ich brauche ein Abführmittel.

Ich brauche ein Schlafmittel.

Ich brauche ein Antazidum.

Ich habe Bauchschmerzen. Haben Sie ein Heilmittel?

Where to Find What You're Looking For

ß (double s), pronunciation of, 17

abbreviations, 204-205
  for German-speaking countries, 147
  railroad, 229
accommodations, 35-36, 156-157
accusative case, 87, 129-130
accusative/dative prepositions, 200-201
accusative prepositions, 199-200
active knowledge of a language, 10-11
adjectives, 95-98, 100-108
  comparative and superlative, 107-108
  demonstrative, 101-102
  game for learning, 97
  list of common, 96-97
  mixed declensions, 105-106
  possessive, 103-104
  practice for learning, 98
  predicate, 98
  strong declensions, 100-101
  weak declensions, 104-105
adverbials, 125
adverbs, 99-100
airports, 154
articles, 71, 82, 85-86
  cases of, 86-88
  see also definite article; indefinite article
associations, 52-53
associative learning style, 10
audio learning style, 10
Austria, 149
Autobahn, worst things to do when driving on the, 33
automobiles, see cars

bakeries, 59, 161-162
bathroom fixtures, 60
be (verb), 110
beer, 61, 153, 234-235
Berlin, 148
Berlitz, Maximilian, 5-6
Berlitz Method, 5
Bierdeckel, 172
birthdays, 137
  cards, 233
bitte, use of, 167
body language, 30-31
brand names, pronunciation of, 19
brauchen (to need), 157
bread, 161-162
breakfast, 34, 36
buffet restaurants, 173
buses, 33
business, 225-227

calendar words, 23-25
cars, 144
  German, 59-60
cases, 86-88, 127-130
  see also declensions
celebrations and special events, 231-232
ch, pronunciation of, 17
chat, online, in German, 58
cheese cake, 176
children, language learning by, 7
chores, list in German for, 57, 61
Christmas, 136-137
church services, 37
classes, German, 56-57
clothing, 37, 181, 183-185
  fabrics, 186
  sizes of, 188-189
cognates, 69-70, 74-75
colloquial terms, 142-144

comparative adjectives, 107-108
compliments, 173
compound nouns, 92
computer programs for translation, see translation programs
conjugations, 110, 122
consonants
  clusters, 19
  pronunciation of, 16-18
  sound shift rules for, 72
conversation(s), 134, 209-218
  asking people where they are from and what they do, 212-214
  easy-to-use structure for, 214
  "fill" words in, 216-217
  getting started with, 209-212
  role-playing in, 217-218
  telephone, 214-215
correspondence, 140-142
cost of things, asking about, 181
countries, names of, 213
courses of meals, 170
credit cards, 143
cuisine, 159
  see also food; meals; restaurants
cultural nuances, 134-135
currency, 138-140
  see also money
curses, 60
cutlery, 166

dairy products, 168-169
Danish, 68
dates
  worst things to do when scheduling, 24
  see also calendar words

dative case, 87, 129-130, 177-179
dative prepositions, 197-198
dative pronouns, 178
days of the week, 24-25
declension paradigm, 86
declensions, 122
  of adjectives
    demonstrative adjectives, 101-102
    mixed declensions, 105-106
    possessive adjectives, 103-104
    strong declensions, 100-101
    weak declensions, 104-105
    see also cases
decoding system, 71-73
definite article, 82, 86
  declension of, 88
demonstrative adjectives, 101
desserts, 34, 175
dialects, 37, 72, 128
  worst things to do with, 139
dictionaries, CD-ROM or online, 246
dinner, 34
diphthongs, 16
directions, asking for, 155-156
direct object, 86-87, 124, 129
discounts, student, 195
dress, 37
dress sizes, 189
drinking, driving and, 33
drinks, 169, 234-235
  beer, see beer
  wines, 235-236
driving, 33
drunk, ways to say you're, 236-237
du (you), 111
dürfen (to be permitted), 113-114
Dutch language, 68-69

eateries, see restaurants
eating utensils, 166
electronic reference tools, 246
emergency services, 224
English
  differences between German and, 127

finding someone who speaks, 42, 138
German's relationship to, 4
inflection in, 122-123
similarities with German, 123
speaking in, 42-44
words "adopted" into German, 75-76
words borrowed from German into, 78-79
entschuldigung (pardon), 31-32
Euro currency, 190

fabrics, 186
fahren (to drive or travel), 151
false friends, 75
fashion accessories, 37
feminine plurals, 85
feminine suffixes, 84
  to make the name of an occupation feminine, 85
"fill" words, 216-217
finger counting, 31
first person, 110
fish, 169
flash cards, 9, 64
flatware, 166
flea markets, 182
food, 160-166
  misleading words, 174
  see also meals; restaurants
Franklin, Benjamin, 39
French, words borrowed from, 77-78
fruits, 168
Fußgängerzone, die (pedestrian area), 199
future tense, 118-119

gender
  of compound nouns, 92
  of nouns, 83-85, 87
genitive case, 87
German Americans, 39, 205-207
Germanic languages, 68-69
gestures, 30-31
Goethe, Johann Wolfgang von, 63
Goethe Institute, 56
goodbye, regional differences in words for, 146
grace, saying, 176
grammar, German, 121-122

awareness training, 123-125
spoken conversation and, 128
terminology of, 122
worst things to assume in, 127
gratefulness, letter expressing, 141
Greek, words borrowed from, 77-78
greetings, 134-135
  casual, 210
  regional differences in, 146
Grimm, Jakob, 71
grocery stores, 163-164
  food items in, 167-169

haben (to have)
  past tense of, 118
  present subjunctive of, 165-166
Hamburg, 147
head gestures, 31
heißen (to be called), 210
hello, regional differences in words for, 146
help, getting, 223-224
herbs, 171-172
High German, 71, 139, 148
hiking, 185
holding memory, 54
holidays, 24-25, 136-137
hotels, 35-36, 156-157
household items, labeling in German, 59

Icelandic language, 69
illness, 237
immersion in German, 8, 59
imperative mood, 111
indefinite article, 90-91
indicative mood, 110
indirect object, 87, 124, 129
infinitive, 110-11
inflection, 86, 122
information, international symbol for, 151
information booth, conversation at an, 139-140
Internet, the, 62
  see also Web sites
interpreters, 44-47, 243-244
itinerary, 195-197, 222

kaufen (to buy), 187
kein, 92-93
Kinesthetic learning style, 10

Konditorei (confectioner's shop), 162
können (to be able), 113-114
kosten (to cost), 181

language acquisition, types of, 5-6
last names, 100
Latin, words borrowed from, 77-78
learning a language
  methods of, 5-6
  worst things to do when setting goals for, 6
learning environment and supplies, 55-57
learning German
  easiest ways of, 7-8
  in immersion courses, 8
  "need-to-know" approach to, 8
  pitfalls in, 45
  questions to answer about, 7
  resources, 247-249
  worst things to do when, 122
learning style, determining your, 9-10
letters (correspondence), 140-142
literature, German, 63
Low German, 71
lunch, 34

machen (to make), 114-115
magazines, 130-131
main dishes, 174
manners, 133
masculine suffixes, 83-84
meals, 34, 135
  courses of, 170
  main dishes, 174
  planning, 173-176
  side dishes, 174
meat, 35, 169
medications, 237
memorizing poems or songs, 63
memory, 54
menu planning, 173-176
menu terms, 167-171
military clock, 153
milk and milk products, 168-169
mixed adjective declensions, 105-106

mnemonic method, 52
modals, combining, 116-117
modal verbs, 112-114
mögen (like to have), 112
money, 138-140
  exchange rates, 190-191
  prices, 181, 190-191
months, 24-25
mood, 110
movies, German, 37-39
Munich, 52, 148-149
  asking for a beer in, 153
museums, 196
music, 11-12, 63
MWS (Mehrwertsteuer), 190

names
  of countries, 213
  of people, 210-212
nehmen (to take), 155
neuter suffixes, 84
news, in English, 50
newsgroups, in German, 58
newspapers, 130-131
nodding, 31
nominative case, 87
nonverbal communication, 29-31
Norwegian language, 69
nouns, 71, 81-82
  articles and, see articles
  cases of, 86-87, 90
  compound, 92
  gender of, 83-85, 87
  plurals of, 85
number, of verbs, 110
numbers, 20-23
  exercise on, 23
  practicing, 23
  punctuation for, 22

objects, 124
  dative, 178
  see also direct object; indirect object
objects of sentences, 86
online chat, in German, 58
online translation engines, 48-50, 245

parlor game, 108
parties, 231-234, 238-240
  small talk, 233
passive knowledge of a language, 10-11
pastries, 34
past tense, 117-118

pedestrian area (die Fußgängerzone), 199
pen pals, 8, 62
permanent memory, 54
pharmacies, 237
phone cards, 216
phrase books, 44
planning your trip, 50, 222
"please" trick, 166-167, 172
plurals, 82
  of definite article, 88
  feminine, 85
pointing, 30
possessive adjectives, 103
practice, 51, 58
predicate adjectives, 98
prefixes, separable, reflexive verbs with, 180
prepositional object, 124
prepositions, 197-201
  accusative, 199-200
  accusative/dative, 200-201
  contractions used with, 201
  dative, 197-198
prices, 190-191
problems, 219-225
pronouns
  dative, 178
  reflexive, 180
pronunciation, 13-14
  of brand names, 19
  of consonants, 16
  tongue twisters, 26
  of vowels, 14-16
Prost, 61, 135
public transportation, 32-33, 196, 227-229
punctuality, 24, 135
punctuation, for numbers, 22
puns, 47

questions, 126, 155-156
  business, 226-227
  everyday, 219-225
  about names, 210-212
  where are you from?, 212-213

radio, traffic advisories on, 204
rail pass, 228
reflexive pronouns, 180
reflexive verbs, 179-181
  with separable prefixes, 180
regular verbs, 115-116
restaurants, 33-35, 140, 159-161

buffet, 173
compliments to the chef in, 173
menu planning, 173-176
menu terms, 167-171
ordering at, 164-166
special requests at, 171
vegetarian, 171
romance languages, 68
rooms, objects found in, 82

safety precautions, 225
saint name days, 137
sales, 190
Sausages, 35, 169
schedules, train, 32, 228
Schwyzerdütsch (Swiss German), 150
scratching head, 31
seasons, 203
second person, 110
sehen (to see), 195
sein (to be), 109, 111
past tense of, 117
sentence construction, 99
sentences, 121-131
patterns of, 126
word order in, 122, 126-128
separable prefixes, reflexive verbs with, 180
shaking hands, 135
shaking your head, 31
shoes, 37
sizes of, 189
shopping, 177-178
sales and discounts, 190
shrugging, 31
side dishes, 174
Sie, 111
sightseeing, 193-207
itinerary items, 196
silverware, 166
sizes of clothes, 188-189
slang terms, 142-144
small talk, 233
smiling, 31
sound shift, 71
souvenirs, 181-183
spelling, 16
spices and herbs, 171-172
spinning, 31
stores
business hours, 187
service at, 187
words you'll need to find, 182

stress (emphasis), 19
stress (pressure), 55
strong adjective declensions, 100-101
student discounts, 195
subjects of sentences, 86, 124
subjunctive mood, 111
of haben, 165-166
subways, 33
suffixes
feminine, 84
to make the name of an occupation feminine, 85
masculine, 83-84
neuter, 84
superlative adjectives, 107-108
supermarkets, 163-164
Swedish, 69
Switzerland, 147, 150

table manners, 135-136
tableware, 166
talking in German, 61-62
to yourself, 62-63
tapping head, 31
tax, value-added, 190
telephone, emergency number, 224
telephone conversations, 214-215
temperature, 204
tense, 110
future, 118-119
past, 117-118
thanks, regional differences in word for, 146
third person, 110
tickets, transportation, 32-33
time
expressions of, 196
telling, 153
tipping, 35, 140
toasts, 135, 233
tongue twisters, 26
tours, in English, 49
trade shows, 225-226
traffic rules, 33
tragen (to wear), 187
train schedules, 32, 228
trams, 33
translation
computerized, 48-50
meanings lost in, 47-48
translation programs, 89, 246
online, 245-246

translators, professional, 44-46, 243-244
transportation, 32-33, 196, 227-229
traveling, 151-153
bummers and bloopers, 220-221
interruptions, disturbances, and surprises, 220
itinerary, 195-197, 222
questions, 221-223
travel papers, 221-222
tutors, private, 55-56

umlauts, 15, 19
understanding German, learning German versus, 6
United States, Germans in, 205-207

value-added tax, 190
vegetables, 168
vegetarians, 171
verbs, 109-119, 124
modal, 112-114
combining, 116-117
reflexive, 179-181
regular, 115-116
that take dative objects, 178
visual learning style, 9
vowels
diphthongs, 16
pronunciation of, 14-16
sound shift rules for, 72-73

weak adjective declensions, 104
weather, 201-204
Web sites
German-language, 62
Goethe Institute, 56
translation programs, 89
Weihnachtsmärkte (Christmas markets), 136-137
wines, 235-236
wollen (to want), 112-113
word order, 122, 126-28
work, asking people where they, 213
working memory, 54

Yiddish, 69
yodeling, 112

Zurich, 150